Contents

CW00544294

About the author and Fiduciam

Dr Sonya Wallbank is the founder and CEO of Fiduciam UK Ltd. As the original developer of the restorative resilience programme of supervision, in 2009, Sonya has maintained a strong belief that resilient staff are much more able to carry out their role effectively.

Sonya is a chartered psychologist by background and an associate fellow of the British Psychological Society (BPS). She is also a registered member of the Health and Care Professions Council (HCPC) and a chartered member of the Chartered Institute of Personnel Development (CIPD).

Sonya is the founder of Capellas Nurseries Group and has worked in the UK, USA and Australia, training a range of staff to utilise her model within their work. Her most recent NHS position was Director of Children and Families. She has trained a range of staff in the NHS, Department of Health, local authorities, private organisations, hospices and charities. As a keen writer, Sonya has published in both professional journals and books and has a number of ongoing blogs.

www.hcpc-uk.org

The British Psychological Society

Fiduciam means 'confidence' and was founded by Sonya Wallbank to work directly with parents as well as professionals working in the social care, health and voluntary sectors to build resilience and confidence in their skills by adopting a positive training approach.

Fiduciam comprises a team of associates, all experts in their own field, delivering training on parenting, safeguarding, mental health, leadership, coaching and restorative resilience. We believe that building someone's confidence in their own method and techniques will enable them to maintain the delivery of their role, even in difficult times. We leave our delegates with insight, education and skills, and always ensure sustainability is built into our training events.

Acknowledgements

Developing the reader and the training pack would not have been possible without the support of hundreds of participants who have experienced the training. Thank you for your time and input into helping us achieve a model that enables you to continue your great work.

I am particularly grateful to Sally Brown, Martin Wallbank, Gavin Spears, Maggie Fisher and Phillipa Bishop, who have worked tirelessly to support both the training programmes and myself to develop the thinking and delivery of the model.

Chapter 1:
Introduction

*'My mission in life is not merely to survive, but to thrive;
and to do so with some passion, some compassion, some
humour, and some style.'*

Maya Angelou

The focus of this publication is on providing information that will be useful to you in understanding why restorative resilience supervision has a positive impact on those professionals who undertake it. It is not designed to be an exhaustive review of the literature in areas such as stress, burnout and clinical supervision, but more a practical guide to enable you to develop a working knowledge of the key theories underpinning the model.

The erosion of resilience

First, we want to consider what the resilient professional looks like and why that resilience is being eroded, creating vulnerability in the workforce. Worker stress, burnout and lack of compassion are frequently reported themes associated with the helping professions. Professionals working within the public and voluntary sectors frequently report the daily pressures that the worker faces. Budgetary restraints, increased public demand for services as well as the changing population demographic means that those working within the helping professions have a heightened vulnerability to stressors. This challenging work environment appears to foster within its workers a resigned acceptance that struggling to manage professional demands is an integral part of this work:

> *'HSE says workers in Health and Social care have some
> of the highest rates of self-reported illness due to stress,
> anxiety and depression.'*

(NHS Employers, 2009, p1)

Given the cost to the public purse, with £300–400 million currently being spent in the NHS alone on sickness pay (NHS Employers, 2009), there is much incentive for organisations to get this right. If workers do not actually go off sick they are also more likely to be experiencing 'presenteeism', where they feel unwell and should really be at home (Rayson, 2011). The way that staff are feeling can result in an increase in accidents, errors, low morale and poor performance, and can also have a significant impact on well-being, productivity and effectiveness (NHS Employers, 2009).

The impact of the environment on the worker is revealed in serious case reviews in which competent, well-trained professionals have demonstrated a reduced capacity to think. This often ends in tragic consequences and stretches beyond professional boundaries:

> 'Missed opportunities to protect Daniel and potentially uncover the abuse he was suffering occurred … In this case professionals needed to "think the unthinkable".'
>
> (Coventry LSCB, 2013, p6)

> 'There are places where unhealthy cultures, poor leadership, and an acceptance of poor standards are too prevalent.'
>
> (Francis, 2013, p25)

While in the event of such tragedies the dominant narratives tend to focus on the failings of the professionals, what seems to be missing is any understanding of why these things happen. Why do we assume that undertaking clinically complex work does not leave its mark on the professional? Why do highly trained professionals miss critical information, accept versions of events that do not correlate with the evidence in front of them or make no sense, and have a reduced capacity to think and challenge? Why are we not ensuring robust support systems are in place which improve and maintain professionals' capacity to think? Instead we choose system changes and drives for efficiency that challenge the capacity of the individual professional to retain their resilience.

In attempting to understand the impact of helping and caring work in all its guises, we will argue that individuals who enter into this field, regardless of professional career choice, have inherently good intentions. While their decisions, or lack of them, may have led to evidence of less than competent practice, our role is to understand how and why this could happen on such a frequent basis.

Rather than produce another set of 'must dos' for those who want to work within clinically complex or challenging environments, this reader challenges the notion that this work can be competently achieved without leaving its mark on the individual undertaking it. It will ask questions about what happens to the thinking style of professionals who are under pressure, and offers some explanations as to why professionals miss critical information, accept versions of events that do not correlate with evidence in front of them or make no sense, and have a reduced capacity to think and challenge.

Professional vulnerability

We will then move to discuss how the absence of resilience and the inherent personality and values of the 'helper' create vulnerability in them. In order to remain emotionally well and engaged within their work, professionals need to understand their own vulnerability and triggers and have a robust method of managing the impact of their work. The psychological responses or reactions of professionals working in the helping or caring professions have been the subject of many research papers. It is important to consider that, while there are professionals who will exhibit severe reactions to their work context, the impact the work is having is not necessarily obvious. Often, professionals attracted to this type of work are coping with their everyday context by struggling quietly and will be displaying less obvious symptoms. This is partly due to the personality traits that are intrinsic to professionals who want to help and care for others – they are carers but can fail to recognise that they also need to be cared for.

These professionals typically also exhibit a high level of functional behaviour, focusing on the work at hand rather than thinking more deeply about it. This is perhaps why individual needs are not recognised – because of the sheer demands of the work, which can make it difficult for those professionals to communicate, 'I need something for me'. Occupational health serves to address the needs of the worker who is simply not coping, but this can be disingenuous to the professional. Being referred to occupational health means that this reaction is considered an individual problem rather than a naturally occurring reaction to the work context or content.

We will explore recognised vulnerability factors (Firth-Cozens & Payne, 1999) within the helping and caring workforce and the impact on an individuals' health of high levels of commitment to their jobs.

In understanding vulnerability, we will then discuss protective factors: what can professionals do to prevent, minimise or overcome the potentially damaging effects of adversity in their work? Adversity in this context is unlikely to be a one-off event, but rather a series of building pressures. It is sometimes what seems to be an insignificant event that has a significant negative impact, and which therefore leads us understanding how little resilience we had left. We will consider the impact of frequent challenging circumstances and how the professional can build a framework to cope with increased expectations and complexity against a backdrop of budgetary restraints and raised client demands.

We will then look at the individual factors that support resilience by increasing a professional's capacity to build trusting relationships within their workplace and emotional connections outside of work to encourage social connectedness. We will also explore the role of workplace self-esteem.

Having identified what makes professionals vulnerable and how they can build resilience and protective factors, we will then consider the role of supervision in the workplace to support professionals, reduce risk and manage caseload interventions.

Stress

We will then move to consider some of the research that has looked at the impact of helping work. We will explore the literature around stress, anxiety and burnout within the helping professions, with a view to considering appropriate interventions. We know that there is much debate regarding sickness levels within the public sector, with a reported 60% higher level of sickness among public sector employees compared to their private sector colleagues (Peacock, 2012).

Although a number of factors have been considered as possible causes for this, such as the average public sector worker being older and therefore more likely to be unwell, or that the workforce is predominantly female and likely to have other caring responsibilities, what appears to be missing is the premise that caring work '…against normal standards can be distasteful, disgusting and frightening' (Menzies-Lyth, 1959). In order to remain emotionally well and engaged with their work, professionals need to understand their own vulnerability and triggers and have a robust method of managing the impact of the work.

Why restorative resilience supervision?

'Managers must recognise anxiety undermines good practice. Staff supervision and the assurance of good practice must become elementary requirements in each service.'

(DCSF, 2009, p7)

While there are numerous studies covering the topic of clinical supervision, the fact that 'supervision' is used as an umbrella term, with little or no clarification around function and purpose (Gonge & Buus, 2011), remains an issue.

In considering here the value of implementing a model of restorative resilience supervision, we discuss the challenges of comparing the model, given the dearth of evidence for supervision models in general. The essential aim of clinical supervision should be to increase the resilience of the professional, ensuring they can act on risk appropriately as well as guaranteeing and improving the quality of care or intervention they are delivering (Wallbank & Woods, 2012). The assumption that supervision is a ubiquitous term, despite the variety of contexts it is practised in, does impact the ability of those practising supervision to understand its essential aims.

The model of restorative resilience supervision was first developed in response to the emotional demands on midwives, doctors and nurses of caring for families who had experienced miscarriage and stillbirth (Wallbank, 2010). The programme was designed to support the professionals to process their workplace experiences and support them to build resilience levels to ensure they had future coping strategies beyond the initial life of the supervision sessions. The impact of the sessions on the professionals' levels of stress, burnout and compassion satisfaction (pleasure derived from doing their job) was measured using the Professional Quality of Life scale (ProQOL) (Stamm, 2008). Results showed that after six sessions compassion satisfaction was improved while stress and burnout reduced by over 40%.

Since the initial studies, the programme has been delivered to over 4,500 professionals (see www.restorativesupervision.org.uk). The model of training has evolved from the sessions being delivered directly by a clinical psychologist to a range of professionals being trained to deliver the sessions themselves. This provides a sustainable model and ensures that the supervision can continue beyond the initial training sessions.

The training model consists of a training day, no more than six individual sessions of individual supervision, followed by small group supervision. The move into group supervision aims to enhance the teamwork capacity of the supervisees and takes place only once they are in a resilient enough state of mind for this process to work well for them. The ongoing effectiveness of group supervision following the individual sessions has also been tested, showing not only how it maintains resilience but also enhances workplace functioning (Wallbank, 2013). The possibility of accessing further limited individual supervision is always kept open, in case a specific event or circumstance arises. Results continue to be consistent, with reductions in stress and burnout and an increase in compassion satisfaction (Wallbank, 2015).

A training pack that accompanies this book is also available from Pavilion Publishing, which provides all the information necessary to introduce restorative resilience supervision into an organisation. It is designed to complement this book and will take you step-by-step through the preparation needed, offering guided instructions for running a training day including a PowerPoint presentation, handouts and demonstration videos of the model in practice, and provides information on rolling out the model throughout an organisation and sustaining it into the future.

For more information or to order a copy, visit: https://www.pavpub.com/restorative-resilience-model-of-supervision-training-pack/

Organisations implementing the restorative resilience model have conducted their own satisfaction surveys with patients and families in their care to review pre- and post-supervision data. The benefits of the supervision model have also extended beyond the supervisors themselves, with higher levels of patient and family satisfaction reported where staff were undertaking supervision (Department of Health, 2013). Staff themselves reported higher levels of satisfaction with the care and interventions they were able to offer. Compassionate care experiences were also more evident (Wallbank, 2015).

Organisational impact has also continued to be measured where the programme has been cascaded. Inappropriate workplace behaviours are more likely to be challenged where the model of supervision has been implemented. Organisational attachment (St. Clair, 2000) – the way in which individuals identify and work collaboratively with their employers – also improves. Sickness levels and turnover of staff decreases and the capacity of the professional to engage with others improves. An inadvertent benefit also appears to be the capacity of the professional to think about their own health behaviours. Some in the study talked about giving up smoking, losing weight or eating more healthily. We know that the sessions enabled the professional to feel more cared for and therefore they felt more able to care for others. This appears to be as a result of the capacity of the professional to slow down their thinking and improve their decision-making. Ultimately, the sessions ensured that professionals were more effective in their work and able to demonstrate their boundaries, and were calmer as a result (Wallbank, 2010):

> '*Ultimately, I feel stronger and I have greater thinking capacity … I also feel valued by my employer for recognising that this is a challenging time.*'
>
> (Trueland, 2013)

The final chapters will focus on the background model of restorative resilience supervision and the evidence that working with over 4,000 professionals has enabled us to gather. We know that maintaining the capacity to think and act in a consistent way when you are under daily pressure is challenging, and we offer a theoretical understanding of why we believe the model of supervision under discussion works. We explore the development of the thinking around the model and the different ways organisations have used the model to sustain a supervisory practice that supports professionals' needs. We will then consider the next steps for researching workplace resilience and the potential benefits restorative resilience supervision has to offer.

Chapter 2:
The erosion of resilience

'Stars may be seen from the bottom of a deep well, when they cannot be discerned from the top of a mountain. So are many things learned in adversity which the prosperous man dreams not of.'

Charles Spurgeon

We begin this chapter by considering how we recognise resilience in a professional and why this is important. What does the resilient professional look like? How do they communicate and behave with colleagues, as well as their clients or patients? We will then review some of the evidence that suggests that resilience is being eroded and consider why this might be. Finally, we will consider what workplaces might be able to do to reverse the decline.

Adversity and challenge will always form part of the helping professional's work context. It could be argued that our experience often mirrors or parallels the very people we are trying to help and therefore by understanding our own reaction to adversity, we learn more about the way we can support others. The challenge is in ensuring that the adversity or stress is not experienced by us as being so great that we are unable to cope with it. In order to achieve a more resilient way of working, then, we need to understand what resilience actually looks like.

What is resilience?

The term resilience is thought to have been first used in the early 17th century and comes from the Latin verb *resilire*, meaning to rebound or recoil. Thomas Tredgold introduced the term in an academic sense in 1818 to describe timber, using the word to explain why some types of wood were able to accommodate sudden and severe loads without breaking. The resilient individual is defined as having '…the capacity to recover quickly from difficulties; toughness' (Oxford English Dictionary, 2015).

The resilient individual is able to experience stress, challenges and adversity, and both cope with these demands and potentially grow from them. When we identify a resilient individual, what is it that we are looking for?

First, emotional intelligence: the resilient professional is able to connect with those around them, including, most importantly, the people they want to help. This connection or engagement is on even terms; they are not overwhelmed by the emotions or demands of others. They have the capacity to reflect back the needs of others, rather than acting like a sponge and taking on board all of the demands of the other person.

Next, the individual is likely to exhibit measured behaviours, especially when faced with stressors. They will be calm and able to think clearly about what needs to be done. They will demonstrate strong and positive problem-solving skills and draw upon the resources of people around them to support them. The strength in their approach is likely to come from a wide group of social support as well as guidance and mentorship from others.

The resilient person is likely to be positively engaged with their workplace. This does not mean that they are not a challenger or a catalyst for change but that they can do this in a constructive manner. They are emotionally intelligent enough to see the perspective of others and this means they are likely to be a positive influencer of change rather than a negative driver of resistance. Where they see things wrong within their work context they will have a wider base of support to draw from to enable changes to take place.

There will also be a positive narrative relating to work when you discuss this with a resilient person. While they are able to accept the challenges and difficulties that the work can present, they balance this with a view of what needs to change and are able to see the positive elements of their workplace. They are not likely to have a wholly idealised view, but are able to offer a balanced narrative that is accepting and also constructively challenging.

As they are able to see the need for practice development, especially in areas that are not performing or meeting objectives, they are open to change and able to accept the requirements on them in order to make this happen. They are likely to be the ones making a proper case for change and demonstrating their willingness to be an early adopter of change rather than resisting the activity. The resilient professional utilises rules and consequences to their advantage, working within a safe framework of governance and responsibility but challenging the system where the rules are interfering with the capacity to provide an effective service.

They are likely to have high expectations of themselves and others, recognising the diversity and abilities of others and demonstrating aspirational behaviour for themselves, their organisations and their client group.

The way in which the resilient professional communicates will be open and honest. While they recognise the impact that they have on others, they will also be able to communicate difficult messages in a sensitive manner. This ensures that they retain positive relationships even in difficult circumstances.

Finally, they will exhibit 'boundaried behaviour'. This means that they volunteer for other activities above and beyond their core role, but are also able to express choice and control over what they take on. They are less likely to feel overwhelmed by their workload or demands as they are more able to discuss the expectations of others before they experience difficulties.

Overall, the resilient individual is probably the one you want to give up your time for and spend time with. They will give off a feeling of energy, and this in turn will give you pleasurable feelings because they will be interested in what your contribution is. We are not suggesting that resilient individuals do not suffer from stressful episodes; it is just that they are more likely to have an armoury to cope with the stress and tend to spend most of their time in a more resilient state.

Where are the resilient individuals?

In describing the resilient individual and how they might behave, you may be left wondering whether it is realistic to expect any professional to maintain a consistently resilient approach in the face of the demands of their job. Perhaps all professionals start out with a resilient mindset but the job content and the work context are not conducive to maintaining this over time?

The 'real' content of helping work is not available for general discussion, mainly because of the distressing nature of the work. Little has changed since Menzies-Lyth's seminal work in the 1950s, where she studied the impact of nursing work on student nurses. Drawing conclusions about the nature of the work, she argued that nurses were exposed to work which was frightening and would be found by others to be disgusting or at least distasteful (Menzies-Lyth, 1959). Who really wants to hear about the emotional, physical or psychological frailty of others? How can we be made aware of the real content of professionals' work in these areas without being made aware of our own frailties? We 'defend against' or put barriers up against learning this intimate knowledge by not entering into discussions about it or by building a picture in our minds that bears no resemblance to reality.

When we think of a doctor or nurse, the image we conjure up is not one of death, dying or suffering, but of a smartly dressed or uniformed individual ready and competent to offer care. This assumption can make raising or discussing the reality of the workplace extremely difficult for the individuals working within the system. There is also an organisational culture where competence of individuals is expected and therefore showing perceived weaknesses or not being able to cope is judged harshly (Francis, 2013).

'While there can be no excuses for poor care, there are often explanations.'

(Royal College of Nursing, 2013)

Those working within social care do not appear to fare any better, although the reality of their work may be a little more evident to the public because of high profile serious case reviews; they tend to be judged as having control and power to 'do' something. When that 'something' is perceived as not being done, the reality of the complexity of the case and the work environment, the uncertainty about what was occurring within the family, and the anxiety of getting it wrong are ignored. Consider the Daniel Pelka serious case review, which asked professionals to 'think the unthinkable' (Coventry LSCB, 2013, p6). Is this a skill that is taught as part of professional training or are we moving towards having our health professionals act in a police or detection role?

It is easier for us to think that something could have been done if only the professionals had been good enough, rather than facing the harsh reality that not all harm can be protected against. We can then put our efforts and resources into the failings of the professionals by 'training or developing' them, or more often punishing them. What seems to be missing is any understanding of why these things happen. We miss questions about how the work impacted on the professional. We do not ask why these highly trained professionals may miss critical information, accept versions of events that do not correlate with evidence in front of them or make no sense, and have a reduced capacity to think and challenge. Instead, assumptions are made that the professionals involved in a case were clearly rogue or not competent (despite the number of cases where things go wrong). The dominant and more comfortable narrative remains that these professionals were bad whereas others are good.

Why are we not ensuring robust support systems which improve and maintain professionals' capacity to think? Instead we choose system changes and drives for efficiency that challenge the capacity of the individual professional to retain their resilience.

All change

Population and societal expectations have increased the demands for helping services tremendously. It now appears to be an accepted fact that the NHS is unable to cope with the demands placed upon it. This news is often reported as if the NHS is an entity that exists outside of the people working within it. The narrative is rarely about how the professionals working within are equally unable to cope with the demands.

While public sector services are continuously reorganised in an effort to deliver even more for less, the emphasis remains on output versus input, and not on whether services are organised in such a way as to protect and promote professionals' resilience. Leaders of efficiency change are not often versed in needing to protect the resilience of professionals, and therefore, while they may deliver the efficiency, we are left with consequences that are negative for the professionals working within the service.

Let's take the drive for open-plan workplaces as an example. This creates a need for less space, promotes hot-desking so fewer computers and desks are required, and means that office space is used more efficiently. What this drive misses, however, is the evidence about how our brain attends to the noise around us even without us knowing, so that rather than being able to stay focused on a task, this environment makes us less productive. It also changes the dynamic of the workplace, meaning limited places to have that debrief conversation or to shut the office door and have a colleague-to-colleague discussion about what is troubling us. As a result, professionals' vehicles become their offices and their usual support systems are eroded along with their capacity to remain resilient.

Another example is the hospital ward: in an effort to speed up the end of shift handover and therefore remove the requirement to have double staffing, handovers are now done at the bedside of the patient. This removes the opportunity for the staff coming on shift to understand some of the subtext about how the patients have been, what their needs are and any concerns they have. There is no debrief opportunity for the staff to express that a shift has been difficult, as they are in earshot of the entire ward. This lack of emotional release is, again, likely to lead to a reduction in resilience.

> 'If you look after your staff, they'll look after your customers. It's that simple.'
>
> Richard Branson

These are just a few examples of how our drive for output has sometimes ignored professionals' needs – and they are delivering the input. Perhaps a workplace context that puts staff and patients/clients at the heart of things is worth considering, especially when designing change.

Creating a resilient workplace

There are a number of actions that are consistently written about within the literature about stress which organisations can implement to ensure they promote a culture of resilience.

Organisational attachment refers to the mental and behavioural attachment of a person to an organisation (Bennett & Durkin, 2000). The organisation should aim to promote the attachment of its employees in order to reduce turnover and because having a positive relationship with your employer is highly protective against stress. An organisation that promotes a strong sense of attachment is more likely to have resilient staff.

In order to experience a sense of strong attachment to an organisation, there are a number of factors that employees consider. The level of commitment to the organisation from the professional is the first key factor. Individuals will gravitate to organisations that are perceived to have high levels of employee commitment. Professionals become interested in working for other organisations when they meet people who are really happy in their work and with whom they work for. Think about the last time you talked about your work: are you an advocate for your organisation or are you significantly less attached?

Organisational values and individuals' level of involvement within the organisation are also important. Having a clear value statement which is written with the involvement of the professionals working within the organisation is highly protective and can foster commitment. The opportunities that staff have to be involved within their workplace and make decisions is also key. This has the additional benefit of encouraging workplace self-esteem and identity, and giving staff a sense of being valued, which are further factors that protect against stress and build resilience.

Employee motivation is another factor affecting attachment relationships. Encouraging appropriate levels of autonomy by allowing professionals to take responsible risks and giving them freedom to act is also protective. This has been shown to increase employee motivation, thereby strengthening professionals' intention to stay with the organisation.

Job satisfaction and the overall attitude of an individual towards their job – and, accordingly, their intention to stay or leave – are also features of organisational attachment. There is a wealth of information written about how employers can improve job satisfaction, but the underlying message is that employees need to retain the hope that things can change in order for them to retain their resilience. If their job satisfaction is low and their organisational attachment is therefore also low, the impact of stressors on them is greater.

The degree to which there is personal integration with an organisation's objectives features prominently in organisational attachment. This is further increased with those working in the helping sector, as we know that personal values feature highly in their reasons for choosing to do such work.

Finally, group coherence, or the way that teams work together, has a consistent bearing on how individuals feel about where they work. The microcosm of the team around the individual can be highly protective against stress and can help build resilience. It can also be a significant stressor for the individual if relationships are not working well. Organisations that pay attention to the functioning of their teams and teach communication and group skills will benefit from higher levels of resilience within their individual staff members.

Chapter 3:
Individual vulnerability

The resilient worker is the ideal, but as outlined in the previous chapter, the demands of working in the health and social care context challenge even the strongest of individuals to remain resilient at all times without support. This chapter will further explain how the content of the work and the organisational context impact on resilience, and explore how these are not the only factors that can increase vulnerability. The individual professionals who are attracted to undertaking this type of work arrive for work with their own inherent vulnerabilities to begin with. Without these vulnerabilities they are unlikely to be successful as a helper or carer, but knowing that who you are impacts on how you are in your work, is a key factor in sustaining resilience.

Why are people drawn to this work?

In order to begin thinking about what makes a professional working in the helping sector vulnerable to stressors, we must first consider what draws them to this type of work in the first place. Individuals who choose helping as career tend to believe more in the kind of the work they do than the pay they receive (Wrzesniewski *et al*, 1997). The meaning and significance that comes from having a higher sense of purpose, and the feeling that one is working towards the greater good, is likely to feature highly in a career choice for this type of individual (Meyer & Herscovitch, 2001).

Working within these sectors is often considered 'a calling'. Those who are drawn to such professions have other employment choices available to them, however, they tend to seek out this type of work. While individuals working within the helping professionals are not a homogenous group, but instead represent a wide range of personality types, these core values of wanting to make the world a better place by helping others, can create vulnerability in individuals (Shanfelt *et al*, 2012). This is because the work requires intense interactions with other individuals in order for it to be achieved. The demands of the work, both in terms of pace and content, can interfere with and disrupt the professional enacting their personal values through their work. If they are too busy to take time to do the work 'properly', as they perceive it, this can be problematic.

The professional gains pleasure and job satisfaction from helping others, and pleasure is protective against stress as it increases the capacity to cope. We will discuss this more in Chapter 5 when we consider how and why we become stressed in the first place. The thought process that we are likely to go through in these instances (which is not necessarily conscious) is likely to be: 'It is busy and my stress levels are raised. I am in demand but I can cope and I am making a difference and enjoying this.'

Feeling that you are doing a good job by delivering good quality care or services mediates against the negative impact of the stressor (Wallbank, 2010). The challenge is the current context, with significant cuts to budgets, ever increasing demands for services and the rising complexity of cases, which do not correlate with delivering the standard of service that many in the helping professions aspire to. Doing a 'good enough' job becomes the accepted norm, with professionals having to redefine what quality means. We know that this compromise has a negative impact on the individual as it reduces their compassion satisfaction (the pleasure they gain from their role). This is not to suggest that the realignment of service delivery is something that the individual professional cannot cope with, just that it has to be thought about and the impact considered. If professionals have choices about the work they do, and they feel that they are unable to perform their role in the way they would like to, they will often leave or retire early (Curtis *et al*, 2006).

The budgetary and performance pressures on organisations within the helping sectors means that conversations about 'core priorities' are constantly revisited. Unfortunately, change is often implemented following limited boardroom discussions because there is no choice about reducing costs. This means that there isn't time to properly consider the consequences for the individuals working within the system. The interaction between the value set of the individual and the perceived morality of the work context are inextricably linked (Bennett & Durkin, 2000). If the professional feels that they are under-delivering care or services where there is a clear need from the person they are helping or caring for, this compromises the worker's capacity to feel good about the work they do.

Given the significance of the value system to the individual professional, when they feel compromised because of how they view their workplace demands or because they feel unable to do a 'good enough' job, their risk of stress is increased.

Who you are

We know that there are specific personality traits that can interfere with work effectiveness and increase vulnerability to stress. The way in which an individual builds relationships, referred to as their 'attachment style', can indicate a higher risk to stressors. 'Anxious or insecure' attachment styles can be defined as:

- being unsure or insecure in relationships with others

- being demanding or possessive
- potentially viewing the independent acts of others as affirmation of their own worthlessness.

This style of attachment has been shown to lead to higher levels of compassion fatigue (Pardess *et al,* 2014). The way in which we 'attach' to others as adults is a result of our early relationship with our main caregiver, over which we will have had little or no control. Identifying the patterns within our current relationships can be helpful in supporting our coping ability.

Having a supportive and functioning social support system around us is one of the most highly protective factors against stress and is consistently cited within the stress literature. The increase in compassion fatigue with difficult attachment styles is likely to be a result of preoccupation with work relationships rather than on the work itself (Pardess *et al,* 2014). This means that there is little mental energy left for the work and raises the risk of stress and burnout.

We also know that those individuals who demonstrate low extraversion (they are less outgoing and focus more on their own thoughts) and low agreeableness (they are more likely to be in disagreements with others, less likely to 'let it go') are also at a higher risk of stress and burnout (Sandoval, 1993). This is linked to the way that individuals utilise their social support and coping systems. If they are less likely to open up and talk to others, they will not have opportunities to share thoughts with them and to mentally process the experiences. If individuals are less agreeable to others, they are likely to be less well supported by their peers and supervisors, and are therefore more likely to be facing challenges alone. Personality styles defined by neuroticism, which have raised levels of anxiety, fear, moodiness, worry, envy, frustration, jealousy and loneliness, are also more at risk from stressors (Wortman *et al,* 2012) for similar reasons.

It is interesting to consider whether personality style arises from intrinsic factors – 'This is who I am at the core of my being' – or whether the individual's role or work context creates extrinsic factors which produce a certain type of personality – 'I have to be strong, controlling and organised to do this job and therefore that is who I now am.' Being able to identify your core personality type is a really helpful way of understanding the impact that your role may be having on you. We know that as we age the constructs that make up our personality change (Wortman *et al,* 2012), so our job role is likely to impact on our core personality traits over time.

The approach we take to our work is also a factor in vulnerability to stress. Within the literature, perfectionism is consistently highly correlated with risk of burnout (D'Souza *et al,* 2011). This means that the more concerned you are about how your work is delivered and received, the more you are at risk from stress and burnout.

Finally, the importance of the way in which you cope as an individual can have significant implications for how vulnerable you are to stressors. We know that humour style or how you laugh about your work is likely to be a significant indicator of how you manage stress. Adaptive humour – the type that enhances friendship and strengthens group relationships – is more adaptive against stress than graveyard humour – black humour and inappropriate joking (Martin *et al*, 2003).

Talking to others rather than venting, or negative reactions (shouting, screaming), is, again, protective against stressors (Wallbank, 2010). Understanding how you cope with situations and your natural method of dealing with stress is something you can take immediate control over.

If you recognise that your coping style is linked to more negative outcomes from stress, then identifying more adaptive coping styles is an easy way to improve your own well-being. We are more likely to adopt the accepted coping styles of the organisations we work within (Wallbank, 2010); therefore, understanding the limitations on the support we receive from our work context is another important factor. If your workplace is unable to offer a more adaptive coping style, then understanding the impact this can have on you as a worker is critical for you to move forward.

How you are

'The greatest weapon against stress is our ability to choose one thought over another.'

William James.

Within the helping professions there appears to be almost an acceptance that doing this work will impact negatively on your own health. Excessive job demands, unrelenting and unrealistic targets, physical and mental challenges, limited break times, working unpaid overtime and taking work home seem to be accepted as normal working practices. The findings from the delivery of the restorative resilience programme are that even the most capable individuals are consistently compromised through these demands. The amount of stress stops being energising for individuals as the demands outweigh their resources or ability to cope and they become less productive.

Two of the questions that we have asked individuals during the research phase of the restorative resilience programme are:

- How would you rate your physical and psychological health?
- How would you rate your day today?

Possible responses are 'terrible', 'poor', 'ok' and 'good'. The small percentage (< 10%) of participants who rate themselves good for both physical and psychological health is concerning (Wallbank, 2010). How can our helpers have the capacity to make others feel more able when they are not caring for themselves?

The way in which shifts are structured in the delivery of helping work also plays a part in the well-being of the helper. Shift work, especially working differing times over a working week, has been identified as a conclusive risk factor for breast cancer, and limited evidence has also been found for different cancers as well as other health risks (Wang et al, 2011).

Further evidence of our limited capacity to put the helper's health first comes from research looking at eating, sleeping and rest/relaxation habits among this workforce. Those helpers experiencing higher levels of stress are less likely to be resting, eating and sleeping properly, which may explain rising rates of obesity within the workforce (Kihye et al, 2012). The failure to put oneself first is often reflective of the core values and beliefs that individuals within the helping sector hold. However, without a degree of self-interest and care, the individual will reduce their longevity in this particular type of work.

The well-being of the professional needs to be a higher priority for organisations in order to enhance individuals' healthy behaviours and support good health (Blake et al, 2011). This emphasis may also help to reduce the continuing rise of health and weight issues within the workforce (Bogossian et al, 2012).

Who you rely on

The content of work in this sector means that, while a supportive social network can mediate the impact of stressors, it can only go some way in supporting the individual professional. The work is often confidential or graphic in its nature and therefore not appropriate for discussion with family or friends, so while social support has a buffering effect (Baum et al, 2012), this type of work can often be a barrier to utilising that social support.

The support of supervisors or line managers has been shown to be particularly useful, as has the role of the supportive workplace (Willemse et al, 2012). What has yet to be explored is the impact of the move towards mobile working, open office sharing and the way in which teams are more likely to be working disparately from each other. Without informal structures for providing support, such as the coffee break and naturally bumping into colleagues at the end of the day, professionals are potentially more vulnerable as they have no opportunity to share their experiences.

Work content

It is interesting that some occupations or fields of care within the helping sector are considered more emotionally demanding than others, often without any evidence or studies being completed into the demands of one workplace over another. There is an implicit misunderstanding of the emotional demands of workplaces and it is often assumed that the 'seen' roles undertaken by professionals are the only functions of the workplace. This means that appropriate support for professionals working within workplaces is often underestimated at best and missing completely at worst.

A good example of this is the maternity setting. Dealing with loss is an intrinsic part of working within this field, and yet it is not always considered a highly emotive setting. While professional bodies representing these areas provide information relating to the varying roles professionals can expect to occupy and experience, the potential impact of working with death and dying is often not considered (see, for example, https://www.healthcareers.nhs.uk/explore-roles/midwifery). The general assumption that maternity settings are positive environments where happy events occur may also provide an incongruent environment for staff to acknowledge the sometimes negative and emotionally demanding reality of their work.

The lack of acknowledgement of the emotionally laden work and often intense interactions with other individuals is what places individuals working within these settings most at risk. They are expected to manage, cope and deal with the emotional demands placed upon them regardless of how difficult they find this. If the workplace's usual method of dealing with difficulties is a referral to occupational health, then this will be the only support mechanism that the individual has available. Although, as we have mentioned earlier, such a referral would suggest that the issues lie with the individual and not the content of the work.

That is not to suggest that individuals do not have the capacity to cope with an emotionally laden workplace, but that the lack of acknowledgement of a workplace as emotionally demanding means that individuals are less likely to be prepared for difficulties or to have functional coping strategies in place to deal with them. As the workload continues to increase, there is less room for the protective behaviours, such as an informal conversation with a colleague, to take place (Lea et al, 2012).

Chapter 4:
The impact of this thing called work

'Too many of us leave our lives – and, in fact, our souls – behind when we go to work.'

Arianna Huffington (2014)

Having considered the challenges around this type of work and individual vulnerabilities, we turn now to thinking about what can happen when the work is too challenging. This chapter will review what we think we know about the experiences of people who work in emotionally demanding professions. I use the work 'think' because the research evidence is far from comprehensive and sometimes the way the research has been carried out means its findings cannot always be relied upon. The first part of the chapter will therefore review the gaps in the research evidence, to enable us to critically consider what we think we know. The second part of the chapter will look at what the research appears to be telling us about the emotional and psychological impact of the work and why we find it hard to give this impact a name.

The emotional impact of the work

There is an undeniable expectation in the helping professions that professionals are required to give of themselves. The variety of roles that individuals undertake mean that this 'giving' takes different forms, but all require the professional to be in close, often personal, contact with other human beings. The content of the work means that this proximity to another person is often occurring at a time when the other person is distressed, overwhelmed and in need of physical, mental or emotional support. Many professions teach workers about professional distance: how to maintain appropriate boundaries and look after their own emotional needs in demanding situations. However, in reality this work cannot be undertaken without leaving its mark. Spending your working life being up close and personal with human distress, in its many guises, is something that cannot be undertaken lightly.

How the work impacts the person and how they react to that impact will be a personal journey. It will depend on their personal levels of resilience (how emotionally able they feel), the support systems they are surrounded by both at home and at work (such as friends and colleagues), and how able they feel to manage the demands of their work (both in terms of their ability and being in the right state of mind to undertake the work). What we want to understand in this chapter is what the impact might look like, how this has been described in the literature and why this is important.

Analysing the research

The responses or reactions of professionals working in the helping or caring professions have been the subject of many research papers. It is important to consider that, while there are professionals who will exhibit severe reactions to their work context, the usual coping style of professionals is to struggle quietly and display less obvious symptoms. This section will review the descriptive labels and/or psychological conditions that have been offered as an explanation for the more severe symptoms, to enable you to recognise the spectrum of reactions and aid your understanding of the impact of helping work.

Within the research in this area there is often a lack of robustness in the methodology used by researchers, which leaves a confused picture about what the phenomenon of the impact actually is (Wallbank & Robertson, 2008). The majority of research in this area adopts what is called a phenomenological stance, in which an individual professional is asked to reflect on their own experiences of themselves and their world. This facilitates a greater understanding of the participant's individual experiences and can provide the researcher with insight into the processes that the participant undertakes in order to assign meaning to the events they are exposed to. The main difficulty with generalising from these research findings is that the data is often personal and may bear little resemblance to alternative constructions of reality as seen by others. Researchers often do not use the more personal findings to build next stage research with larger numbers of people.

The research tends to use focus groups, interviews or diaries as a means of data collection. Often, there is a lack of information relating to the methodology used for data collection and therefore the quality of collection is difficult to judge. It is also often unclear how the researcher has used prompts to encourage the conversations. Brocki and Wearden (2005) discuss the influence of using 'minimal probes' – for example, 'how did you feel about that?' or 'tell me more.'

The researcher in the group is also likely to have a different role outside of the research, for example they may be a colleague or manager of the individuals they are interviewing. Their day job role will impact on the reliability of the data – are you likely to tell your colleague or manager the same things you would tell an independent researcher? It is important to understand the responses of the researcher in directing the discussions, as these could change the content of the researcher's findings. This is not to mean that we should just dismiss individual accounts, but we should be aware that in trying to build robust interventions within organisations, a collection of individual and specific accounts may not generate an accurate overview of what is occurring.

The majority of the research is carried out retrospectively, therefore relying on professionals' memories to build a picture of their experiences. The memory of these experiences is likely to be influenced by priming; that is, the events, signals and sounds that are occurring within the group. If you are discussing a topic within the group and others around you are shaking their heads, you are likely to finish what you say much quicker with less detail and depth (Keuler & Safer, 1999). Having a balanced view of the impact of events is difficult if the impact is downplayed or exaggerated as a result of group events.

As we have described, researchers are often colleagues or supervisors who are linked in some way to the respondents taking part. The relationship between the researcher and the data generated is often unexplored and thus it is difficult to know how this has influenced the data generated. It is therefore our starting position that, in order to understand what is happening to professionals who are impacted by their work and to identify what can be done to support them, much greater research efforts need to be made.

Certainly within health settings, findings in the Francis report (Francis, 2013), which studied the reports and events surrounding the Mid-Staffordshire NHS Foundation Trust, have led to a rise in the compassionate care agenda. The report recognised the failings of the organisation to understand the demands of the work on its staff and how this was negatively impacting their ability to care for others. This was not limited to this one organisation, and the report challenged the wider context of the NHS to consider how it could improve performance in this area. This represents the recognition that, if we want professionals to provide a compassionate, connected and personal care experience, then we need to accept that this will have an impact on the person providing that care. In providing excellent quality care, staff need to have their own needs met so they are able to deliver within the most challenging circumstances. While the importance of supporting the staff member is becoming more recognised, the answers to how we do this, especially given the enormity of the organisations providing care, are currently in their infancy.

Professionals' responses

There are a number of subjective descriptors that the research uses to describe the physical responses people have to work events. It is interesting that often the researchers will assign a label based on a cluster of symptoms, despite their being numerous alternative descriptors that could be applied. There is also a high level of subjectivity and assumption around the internal state of an individual based on observable or described symptoms. For example, a nurse who has been exposed to the death of an infant during a 'routine' delivery is described by researchers as experiencing a 'grief' response, based on the described symptoms of distress, crying, and feeling overwhelmed and helpless or angry (Wallbank & Robertson, 2008). 'Grief' as a bereavement reaction, however, is described as a *response to the loss of someone or something that one is strongly attached to*' (Colman, 2001) and may therefore not be an accurate descriptor in this context.

Other feelings reported in response to work events include helplessness, frustration, disbelief and ambivalence. Feeling slowed down and drained as well as not being able to think clearly or make decisions are other common descriptors. One common theme in the literature is that, where professionals are aware that they are being impacted by their work, the emotional symptoms can be short in duration but the psychological impacts more persistent. They tend to endure and resonate long after the trigger or set of events that may have started the reaction.

Professionals experiencing work related difficulties will attempt to control what is going on. The controlling of emotions appears to feature highly under their perception of 'professional behaviour', and as such the individual often dismisses their emotions or considers themselves weak as a result of what they are experiencing. Emotions are considered to be inappropriate and therefore not easily expressed to others. As a consequence, within the caring professions, staff members may focus solely on the physical care of a patient to the detriment of the patient's (and their family's) emotional well-being, despite their need for both. It is as if the professionals are no longer able to care emotionally as they feel too overwhelmed to do so (Wallbank, 2010). There is often a reliance on protocol and procedure and, where such guidance does not exist, it appears that this can increase the reaction from the professional.

The findings from the Francis report (Francis, 2013) demonstrate the negative impact that this has on patient care. The report found that professionals were not offering optimum care and were emotionally withdrawing from their patients. We know that withdrawal from the patient is especially prevalent when there has been a bereavement or loss that has challenged the professional (Wallbank & Robertson, 2008). While putting some emotional distance between the professional and patient is protective for the worker, patients experience this as poor care. It is also counterintuitive for the professional to withdraw in order to protect themselves, as providing a positive care experience was found to be highly protective for the professional against a 'stress' or 'traumatic' reaction to events (Wallbank & Robertson, 2013).

Coping

Professionals do have coping strategies in place to help them attend work and engage in a demanding role despite negative experiences. However, some of these strategies are more effective than others. Using other people for support is a common theme within the literature: creating distance by talking the events through, rationalising them or acting them out to another are all ways of coping with events.

Self-awareness is also identified as a protective coping mechanism – taking time out, praying, reflecting and seeking closure are all ways of dealing with specific events.

Another coping mechanism employed by individuals reacting to negative events is simply taking time off and away from the workplace to begin a process of recovery. However, while this is a positive step for the individual, we know that the trend of sickness and absence within the public sector means that often pressure is increased on those staff who remain at work (Peacock, 2012).

When it comes to coping, organisations themselves have an important role to play. However, they are often considered both sources of support and challenge for staff. Research tells us that collegiate support, having the time and resources to do a job properly and having an opportunity to discuss events are all considered protective by the individuals themselves. Organisations who are able to support individuals in difficult times in a relevant way often find that the 'attachment' to them as an employer increases (Wallbank, 2010), meaning that professionals are more likely to talk about the organisation in positive terms and consider recommending them to others.

Conversely, and sadly, organisations can also provide a negative environment for their staff. Perceptions of professional impotence or not being able to make decisions, lack of knowledge, skills or experience within the team, and perceptions of incomplete services or care delivered, all appear to increase the negative impact of the work on the individual.

How are the responses described?

The following sections consider how the negative reactions of staff are described within the research literature using psychological conditions and their labels to aid our understanding. While these descriptions are useful for us in attempting to understand what is happening and how we can support staff, we begin to see that a number of assumptions are made about the experience in order that it is able to fit the descriptor used.

Post-traumatic stress disorder

While professionals' physical and psychological reactions are varied, there have been some attempts to draw these into a coherent theoretical framework. Some studies discuss the 'trauma' of the work and provide a narrative for interventions more akin to the way one would respond to a victim of a catastrophic event. One of the descriptors used is post-traumatic stress disorder (PTSD) leading to symptoms such as:

- hyper-vigilance (being on guard)
- intrusiveness of thoughts/flashbacks
- avoidance (both in thinking about the event and in physically returning to where the events happened)
- physical symptoms, for example, muscle aches, headaches, stomach upsets.

It is important to note that PTSD can occur as a result of experiencing traumatic events as well as from the fear of possible, future events. That is, even events such as a near miss can be so frightening that the individual has an adverse reaction. Furthermore, professionals do not necessarily have to experience the events directly for themselves, but may have cared for or supported an individual who has experienced a traumatic event. This secondary trauma, or vicarious traumatisation (Figley, 1995), is used to describe reactions that are similar to PTSD but caused by being exposed to individuals who have experienced trauma.

While this may describe the shock and aftermath of dealing with horrific events, even through a third party, it does not help us understand the 'slow burn effect' of some work conditions. It is not just the impact of a one-off event that causes an adverse reaction in an individual, but sometimes an accumulation of events over time. In some cases, in fact, the trigger event can seem entirely innocuous to the outside world.

Emotion work

The term 'emotion work', which relates to Hochschild's (1983) description of emotional labour, is the act of attempting to change an emotion or feeling so that it is appropriate in a given situation. As an example, professionals within the helping sector may be exposed to horrific, scary or distressing events. They may also simply be listening to someone recount such events. In an attempt to calm their patients down or manage the emotion of another, they may downplay their own reaction to the events, despite in reality also feeling scared, anxious or distressed. The research in this area originally began by studying air hostesses and how they would have to appear happy and helpful regardless of what was happening. The term certainly describes the pushing away of negative emotions that appears to happen frequently with professionals who feel they need to 'act' in a certain way. The emphasis of emotion work is on the ability to supress or induce certain feelings according to organisational or professional roles, and this resonates strongly with what happens in practice.

This is a useful concept in describing the process that may be occurring when a professional reacts to adverse events. It also highlights the fact that, in attempting to act appropriately in a situation, the professional is required to actively manage their emotions, which takes effort and is often without reward. The descriptive process, however, has limited use when we consider what an appropriate intervention might be.

Mood disorders

Some studies refer to adverse reactions as mood disorders, such as anxiety and depression, especially where the professional may have had previous vulnerabilities to this type of disorder. In this context, the feelings of anxiety relate to the work events and professionals find it hard to control their worries. The feelings of anxiety are constant and these worries can often cross into all other areas of the person's daily life. Depression is described as severe, often prolonged feelings of despondency and dejection. These feelings are unlikely to be limited to perceptions of work but will impact on all areas of life. While these terms may offer a description of the effect that the environment or events have had on the individual, in order to ensure that we intervene appropriately and with the right individuals, we need to have a more comprehensive framework for understanding why some professionals are more at risk than others. We discuss in Chapter 3 the concept of vulnerability in relation to resilience and how this can guide us to ensure we identify those who may be at risk from mood disorders as a result of their work.

Of the potential theoretical constructs to describe the impact on staff, the most widely researched in the available literature are constructs around stress, burnout and compassion fatigue/satisfaction (Figley, 1995).

Stress

Stress has a number of theoretical explanations, which are explored in more detail in the next chapter. Stress as a theory, however, appears to offer a more encompassing approach than the simple descriptors used earlier to describe the continuum of impact that professionals appear to suffer.

Stress is described as a feeling of being under too much mental or emotional pressure, a pressure that the individual feels unable to cope with. Importantly, people have different ways of reacting to stress and what is perceived by one person as a stressful event may not be stressful to another; it could even be energising for them. Under-stimulation (not getting enough stimulation) can be perceived as just as stressful as over-stimulation through pressure.

Burnout

Burnout is a psychological term used to describe a particularly long-term impact associated with feelings of exhaustion and diminished interest in the workplace. Burnout can be considered as the end point of experiencing too much workplace stress for too long. If stress is the response to the demands or excessive pressures placed upon a person, then burnout is a product of prolonged stress. This allows us to begin to think about the professional's response to their workplace demands as being on a continuum.

Compassion satisfaction and fatigue

Compassion satisfaction (the pleasure one derives from their work) and compassion fatigue (a deterioration over time of the capacity to care for others) (Figley, 1995) are both important when looking at the response from workers in a care or helping environment. The pleasure that a job evokes within a professional is highly protective against the impact of stress and burnout, and is certainly a common trait in those who are attracted to work in these areas. Compassion satisfaction describes the positive feelings that professionals can feel as a result of what they do. It is a generalised feeling of satisfaction when the professional sees how the care or intervention they have delivered impacts on the person they are helping or supporting. These pleasurable feelings bring a sense of fulfilment and well-being to the helper, which motivates them to continue their work even in the face of adversity and stress.

Professional experience and feeling competent in a particular role increases compassion satisfaction (Harr, 2013). Where the professional is in a role that maximises their abilities and they have realistic expectations of what they can achieve, they are also likely to have high levels of compassion satisfaction. In social work, research has found that a supportive work climate positively impacts compassion satisfaction because it encourages relationships, mutual learning and self-care (Harr, 2013).

Compassion fatigue, on the other hand, is a particular type of burnout which effects those providing care to others. It has been widely researched.

'Compassion fatigue is a state experienced by those helping people or animals in distress; it is an extreme state of tension and preoccupation with the suffering of those being helped to the degree that it can create a secondary traumatic stress for the helper.'

(Figley, 1995, p35)

When professionals are not focusing on their own health and well-being, their capacity to care and be attuned to others' emotions can be eroded. This fatigue or inability to care and show appropriate empathy is often associated with other more destructive behaviours, such as apathy, isolation, emotional coldness and using coping techniques that harm overall well-being (for example, substance abuse).

Compassion satisfaction is correlated with lower levels of compassion fatigue and burnout (Harr, 2013). The emphasis in intervention for compassion fatigue should be proactive and focus on increasing the professional's compassion satisfaction (Harr, 2013).

Guiding intervention

While professionals can experience any or all of the reactions to workplace events described in this chapter, it is important to understand the different descriptors that are used, as this will guide the type of intervention you need to offer. Where a professional is diagnosed with a psychological condition, it is not appropriate to intervene unless you are a qualified mental health professional. It is therefore important that, as a supervisor, you understand the range of conditions, so that you can see where you are able to intervene and where you need to seek more specialist support for an individual. Usual models of support and supervision are not appropriate for individuals experiencing PTSD, anxiety or depression, and it is therefore necessary to ensure that these professionals have access to specialist support. For the most part, professionals are less likely to exhibit responses of the severity described here; instead they are usually quietly struggling to cope.

The lack of clarity within the research is important because without a theoretical model of what is possibly occurring, organisations are struggling to provide an appropriate intervention to support their staff teams. Over years of research into the impact of the restorative resilience model, a common theme has been the lack of response from organisations in ensuring that professionals have the thinking capacity to be at work. Rather than assume that this is a consequence of undertaking this type of work, services to support professionals are often placed within occupational health departments and start with the premise that the problem lies with the individual professional rather than the work content or context. Given the demand on individuals working in this area to remain competent, in control and unaffected by their work (Wallbank, 2010), and organisational contexts that often demand similar levels of control, it is easy for professionals to see the need for support as a reflection on their inability to cope.

Chapter 5:
Understanding stress

The previous chapter considered some of the more extreme responses to workplace demands that professionals working within the helping sector can experience. We will now move onto the research surrounding stress.

Stress as a concept or label has taken on a variety of meanings in recent years ('Sally's job is stressful,' 'Simon was acting stressed,' 'They were signed off work with stress'). It is usually connected to a negative experience and suggests maladaptive behaviours to an environment or circumstances. This chapter explores the different aspects of stress as a natural response to the environment, as it is not always a negative experience and some stress is good for us, helping us thrive in an environment.

A key underpinning theory for the restorative resilience model is the understanding that it is our response to the stressor that determines its impact on us, not necessarily the stressor itself. Understanding the positive aspects of stress and how to work to improve an individual's capacity to tolerate stress means you can intervene to reduce its impact.

What happens to our bodies under stress?

Our bodies' stress response occurs when we perceive ourselves to be under threat, a function that evolved to ensure that we have the best possible chance of survival when faced with a life-threatening event. When such responses first developed, far back in our evolutionary past, they were 'designed' to galvanise us for action against direct threats such as predators, to prepare us to fight or to flee. The problem for us arises today because, while our bodies react as they always have done, we are no longer responding to the same threats – the stressors we experience are no longer in the form of dinosaurs, but a demanding boss or a pile of paperwork. Our bodies struggle to cope with this discrepancy between a stress reaction that is geared towards physical action on the one hand, and the nature of the threats we encounter, which rarely require a physical response, on the other.

Let's first look at some of the brain systems that control our stress responses. The limbic system in the brain is a group of structures associated with emotions and drives. It consists of the amygdala, the hippocampus regions of the limbic cortex and the septal area. The limbic system is responsible for connections with the hypothalamus, thalamus and cerebral cortex. The hippocampus is important in memory and learning, while the limbic system is central in the control of emotional responses.

This is the 'alarm system' for the entire body, and it seeks to ensure maximum survival for the individual by controlling our responses to threat. When we perceive a threat, the information is sent from our eyes or ears, for example, through to the amygdala (a primitive area of our brain), taking on average 12 milliseconds to be received (it is worth noting that this compares to 25 milliseconds for information to be sent through to the neocortex, which is involved in higher functions such as sensory perception, generation of motor commands, spatial reasoning, conscious thought and language). The information received by the amygdala is not processed or in-depth, but rather 'quick and dirty', in order to enable a swift and powerful response. The subsequent actions evoked by the system – the stress reaction – are primitive in their nature and hard to control.

Once our brains have decided that a threat exists and evokes the stress response, nerve signals are sent down our spinal cords to our adrenal glands, prompting the release of adrenaline. This chemical increases our heart rate, pumping more blood to our muscles so that we are able to make a quick escape, and also acts to supress pain, among other things. You may be familiar with this as the 'fight, flight or freeze' response, which describes the impact of adrenaline on the body, ensuring you have the physical power if you want to fight or run away. At the same time, the brain sends signals to your pituitary gland at the bottom of your brain, which tells the adrenal cortex to produce cortisol. We know that cortisol ensures that blood sugar and blood pressure continue to remain high to support the stress response. Once in the brain, cortisol remains much longer than adrenalin and it continues to affect brain cells (Talbot, 2007).

Kahneman (2011) distinguishes between our usual thinking patterns, what he calls 'system 2 thinking', and the patterns we experience when under threat/ stress, 'system 1 thinking'. The former pattern is a slower, more considered approach, in which we attempt to find finer details and to build a larger picture of events in order to make decisions. The speeds at which these thought processes occur range between 12 milliseconds for system 1 thinking and 45 milliseconds for system 2, with our subconscious functions taking on a lot of the processing. When we perceive ourselves to be under threat our brains shift into the primitive system 1 thinking. We don't take in details or pause for reflection, but make quick assumptions and conclusions.

It is interesting to consider the impact on our decision-making if we consistently find ourselves operating in a system 1 state. The over-secretion of stress hormones, which happens when we are in a constantly stressed state, has been identified as having an adverse impact on brain function. Sustained stress damages the hippocampus, the part of the limbic brain that is central to learning and memory, and operating in a 'stressed' mode means slower and less effective functioning (Talbot, 2007).

The impact of these biological responses is evident in our experience of delivering restorative resilience supervision. Stress manifests itself in difficult work behaviours, such as:

- lateness
- absence
- low morale
- relationship difficulties
- decreased productivity
- avoidance of emotional involvement
- lack of motivation
- feeling overwhelmed
- reluctance to engage
- difficulty in decision making
- burnout and compassion fatigue.

(Wallbank, 2010)

The impact of disordered thinking as a result of stress, or lacking the capacity to think clearly and make decisions, is evidenced in increased conflicts, accidents and patient/user dissatisfaction, which can lead to a rise in complaints (Wallbank & Robertson, 2008). In the worst cases, it can be responsible for serious incidents or lead to staff burnout and the responses discussed in Chapter 4.

Why stress as a description is preferred

As we demonstrated from the previous chapter, the negative responses of professionals working in demanding environments vary. When these are studied in detail, researchers assign a theoretical framework or label such as 'burnout', 'trauma' or 'compassion fatigue' in order to help the reader understand what is actually being studied. Once this description or label has been applied then assumptions are made about what intervention would be helpful. As an example, the original research into the efficacy of clinical supervision to support staff studied whether restorative supervision mediated the impact of pregnancy loss, stillbirth and neonatal death on the professional in the context of obstetrics (Wallbank, 2010). This research found that previous studies had described the responses from staff as 'grief', despite the distress manifesting in a number of ways. Professionals working in the area did not accept this term as a meaningful description of what they were experiencing and in some cases found it a challenging term given the grief of the parents they were encountering.

Grief was being used within the literature as a generic term to suggest a strong reaction to the situation and feelings such as:

■ distress

■ anger

■ helplessness

■ frustration

■ being overwhelmed

■ disbelief

■ ambivalence.

These emotional states were all being explained by this one descriptor, grief, but it was not clear whether this was describing the emotional state of the professional or the process involved. This was particularly unhelpful for the professionals who were then offered a whole range of interventions from aromatherapy sessions to grief counselling in order to deal with their assumed state.

Stress as a theoretical concept is different from other descriptors because it explains the continuum of responses. Not all events are perceived as stressful and some do not impact on the professional at all because they have good coping mechanisms in place. We consider this next in more detail with a particular model of stress as an example.

Lazarus and Folkman's model of stress

Considered to be one of the most robust frameworks, the transactional model of stress developed by Lazarus and Folkman (1984) focuses on how an individual experiences a stressful event and the cognitive processes that are thought to occur.

The model in Figure 5.1 identifies two processes:

■ cognitive appraisal – a thought process, not necessarily conscious, which leads to…

■ an interpretation of the event – is it stressful?

This is then followed by a process of attributing the causes of the stressful event, and finally we make a secondary appraisal to determine if we have the resources to cope with it. Where the individual believes that they do not have the resources to cope with the stressor, emotional arousal occurs.

Both of these processes are critical mediators between the events experienced by the individual and their perception as to whether they are stressful or not.

Perception and appraisal

Cognitive appraisals made by staff under pressure are highly significant in determining whether they will have a negative reaction to the events experienced (Wallbank, 2010). The way that individuals cope with situations leads to a mediating or exacerbating effect of the impact. Negative appraisals can vary but may consist of worries about:

- how they will cope
- what their colleagues will say about them
- whether they might lose their job
- whether events might overwhelm their emotions
- whether the care or service they give is good enough
- the amount of experience they have – feeling ill-equipped to cope
- the amount of knowledge they have – not knowing enough
- whether they feel they have enough time to do a good job
- other competing demands.

Figure 5.1: Illustration of Lazarus and Folkman's stress model

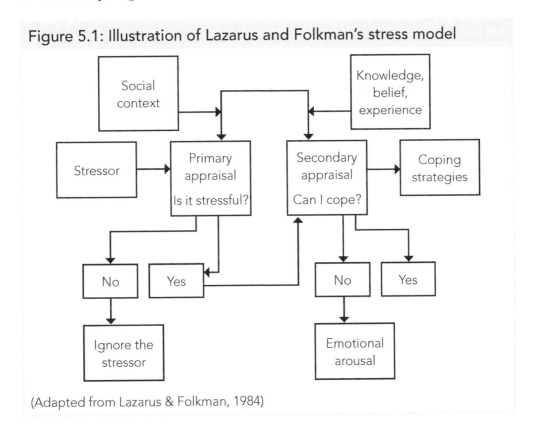

(Adapted from Lazarus & Folkman, 1984)

Box 5.1: An example of Lazarus and Folkman's (1984) stress model in action

Daniel works in a busy department that is short staffed following reductions in its numbers, and there is little or no collegiate or managerial team support for each other. Daniel has not worked in the organisation for long and is used to having a team around him to provide support for the work that he does. The team he works in are community based and they spend a lot of their time out and about as the organisation encourages mobile working. He identifies himself as being junior in experience compared to his colleagues and is feeling a little lost in his current role.

While seeing one of his clients, Daniel is confronted by his client's partner who is aggressive and under the influence of alcohol. The partner begins to attack Daniel's client and, in defending his client, Daniel is also physically assaulted. The police are called and an internal investigation begins. Daniel returns to work but overhears a colleague saying that he should not have gone into the home alone as there is a history of violence from this individual.

Daniel experiences a range of stressful symptoms that day, including a panic attack on the way to see his next client. His GP agrees that he should take some time off work.

Let's consider Daniel's circumstances within the context of the stress model. Daniel's colleagues are not available to support him as they are busy and short staffed. This is not an unusual scenario, with the rise of mobile working, professionals can be physically unavailable to each other as well as mentally.

Daniel believes himself to be junior and therefore questions whether he has the key knowledge, skills and experience to cope with the events he has experienced. This may indeed be an accurate assessment of himself, but it also undermines his capacity to cope. With the lack of mentorship and social support available to him, he is more likely to be vulnerable to questioning himself. Hearing his colleague identify his lack of experience as a factor will resonate deeply with him and confirms his own perception of his vulnerability. Daniel then appraises this situation and potential future situations as highly stressful as he knows that his own capability is unlikely to change in the future and he will remain with little or no support.

Daniel's usual coping strategy would be to seek out others who are more experienced. However, because this strategy is not available to him, this may have led him to perceive the events as overwhelming, ultimately leading to the panic attack and avoidance of the workplace.

One aspect of appraisal is the consideration of our own responsibility. The way in which we think about our role in 'causing' negative events to happen is a significant factor in our ability to cope and deal with situations. Attribution theory (Weiner, 1985), which is concerned with how individuals think about events that have happened to them, applied within care and helping settings, suggests that individuals who explain negative events using internal (self-blame) and controllable ('it is my fault because I did not...') attributions are more at risk of experiencing negative impact (Weiner, 1985). This suggests that professionals who blame themselves or believe that things could or should have been done differently are more at risk from subjective stress. This could be to do with the feelings of guilt that thinking in this way often evokes.

Evidence of a stress model

Inside and outside of the hospital setting, there are a number of studies which utilise a stress model to explain the reactions of staff to stressors (such as the loss of a child or patient) (Wallbank & Robertson, 2008). This body of literature also acknowledges the importance of cognitive appraisals (what the individual thinks is happening) as contributing to the professionals' perception of the event. Negative appraisals, such as the professional being able to identify with a deceased person or their family, or feeling that they should have saved a child, have been identified as strongly associated with increased psychological disturbance for the professional.

Additional evidence across settings also highlights the importance of the work environment, particularly supervisory support, in mediating the impact of events on staff members. This literature points to the particular vulnerability of inexperienced members of staff, suggesting that experience can be protective. We found during the original research that, while inexperience is certainly associated with a raised risk of not coping with stressors, high levels of experience can often lead to overwhelming role demands and therefore less cognitive capacity to manage the stressor (Wallbank, 2010).

Using this knowledge to support intervention

It is useful to consider the stress model and how it might guide interventions with a professional who is suffering stress as a result of their work. We know that the capacity of the individual to cope is significant in determining how they will react to the event or series of events. If an individual has the capacity or resources to cope they will avoid the impact. Increasing a professional's capacity to cope by developing their positive coping strategies will therefore be significant in reducing the impact of stress. We tend to observe that professionals who are at risk of negative stress responses are the individuals who are dedicated to their role, consistently going above and beyond the call of duty until they burn out or have limited energy left to give. Developing a strengths-based, resilient response will ensure staff remain able to cope despite the stressors, as they learn to develop boundaries for themselves.

Professionals often rely on more negative coping strategies, which can cause an increase in psychological symptoms. One interesting finding from the formal research studies that the author was involved in, was that often the professional was not aware that the coping strategies they were adopting were putting them at higher risk. Staff are significantly more likely to adopt negative coping strategies if their work environment, particularly supervisor support, is lacking (Wallbank, 2010).

Negative coping can include:

- venting
- release of negative emotion
- substance use
- self-blame
- humour – particularly 'graveyard or black humour'
- disengagement
- denial
- behavioural and/or mental disengagement.

The stress model (Lazarus & Folkman, 1984) can be used to explain why an individual finds an event stressful or not, how they weigh up their coping capacity and what their response will be. It also offers a framework for considering the different responses that may occur and the type of response that would be most suitable. In order to reduce stress responses we need to find ways to increase resilience, and therefore coping, or to reduce the individual's perception of something as a stressor in the first place.

Chapter 6:
Using supervision as a protective factor

We will now look at how we intervene and work with individuals whose roles expose them to stress. The next chapter will discuss the specific model of restorative resilience supervision, so we first need to begin to understand supervision in more detail.

Why 'supervision'?

We know from the literature researching stress and coping that the concept of 'support', whether it comes from family, supervisors, managers or colleagues, provides a protective experience against stressors. Owing to the nature of helping work, being confidential and/or graphic or psychologically disturbing in its content, it is not appropriate to utilise family or friends to process workplace experiences. Strong and positive relationships with supervisors have been identified as helping to ease the effects of job demands by providing support, understanding and alternative perspectives (Bakker & Demerouti, 2006).

A more formal structure of support needs to be provided within the workplace for professionals. This is required to support and enhance their coping skills by allowing them to reflect on and learn from these experiences, while ensuring that appropriate confidentiality and governance are maintained. It is also important that the provision of such support is delivered by individuals who have an appropriate skillset. This ensures that the support remains effective while an emphasis is kept on the purpose and objectives of the space provided. Clinical supervision has been shown to be able to increase nurses' sensitivity towards themselves and the families they care for (Jones, 2006)

It has also been noted that nurses who attend clinical supervision have an increased level of satisfaction with their psychosocial work environment, through increased job satisfaction and well-being (Begat & Severinsson, 2006). In attempting to clarify the benefits of clinical supervision, the restorative element has been regarded as an essential ingredient to increase job satisfaction and vitality, and reduce stress and emotional exhaustion (Gonge & Buus, 2011).

However, very few studies comment on what actually occurs in a supervision session or what model of supervision staff are being exposed to (Howard, 2008).

In determining what this support should or could look like, organisations appear to be in a constant state of reinvention, especially concerning the role of clinical supervision. Models currently adopted within the UK have been identified as unlikely to be evidence-based and range in the quality of delivery (Wallbank, 2010). This may be less to do with the pace of change and development within organisations and perhaps due to the lack of definition about the practice of clinical supervision itself.

What we do know is that clinical supervision is frequently written about as a 'good thing', but that this tends to rely on more experiential accounts than testing against a rigorous framework. 'Clinical supervision' needs to be treated as a generic theoretical term, such as 'therapy' or 'practice', rather than being described as a specific entity. The specifics of how you choose to conduct the supervision are dependent upon the outcomes you are trying to achieve.

What is supervision?

The term 'clinical supervision' is in itself misleading, with 'supervision' being defined as: 'The action or process of watching and directing what someone does or how something is done' (Collins Dictionary, 2014).

Clinical supervision is not a clinical practice that is 'solely an action or process of reviewing what someone is doing.' The term, therefore, may not have been useful from the outset. This has certainly been the case with the author's experience of working with the medical profession where any form of 'supervision' is deemed to mean the act of measuring performance or competence. This can provide an artificial barrier to the effectiveness of clinical supervision within settings where the purpose and objectives are mismatched against the descriptive term.

Within the helping sector, supervision has come to mean a guiding form of reflection rather than a directive form of managerial control. However, the ubiquitous use of the term to describe a whole host of activities with varying forms and content has been unhelpful in both defining the purpose and methodology of clinical supervision. The myriad uses of the term has also meant that 'clinical supervision' is hailed as the solution to most problematic areas. Various governmental and inspection reports continue to cite clinical supervision as if it is a commonly understood concept. The calls for clarity around function and purpose are frequent (Gonge & Buus, 2011) as is the call for empirical evidence around its effectiveness (Buus & Gonge, 2009; Vlachou & Plagisou, 2011; Wallbank, 2010).

Without being clear regarding the purpose of the supervision activity, there is little benefit in measuring whether it has been effective or not, as we cannot be sure what needs to be measured. Attempts to define the practice have been made by both government and professional bodies, for example:

'Clinical supervision is: a formal process of professional support and learning which enables individual practitioners to develop knowledge and competence, assume responsibility for their own practice and enhance consumer protection and safety of care in complex clinical situations.'

(DH, 1993, p1)

'Clinical supervision is also important as a tool to support you with elements of clinical governance in the following ways:
- *quality improvement*
- *risk management and performance management*
- *systems of accountability and responsibility.*

(Royal College of Nursing, 2014)

'Clinical supervision is designed to discuss work-related issues and for purposes of reflection and monitoring. A relationship of mutual trust, respect and integrity which models best practice and sensitivity to the learning needs of the supervisee.'

(British Psychological Society, 2008).

These definitions demonstrate both the use and misuse of the phrase. Can one intervention really be effective at everything from governance to education without adjusting the content or delivery of the sessions? The statements about the purpose of supervision do not provide any caveats to suggest that the function of supervision is reliant upon the way in which it is delivered. While there are common elements of practice involved in all supervision types, there are also specific differences which need to be acknowledged and more explicitly outlined when researching or commenting on 'supervision.'

In considering the value of implementing a model of restorative resilience supervision, the dearth of evidence around supervision models in general challenges how you compare the effectiveness of this model with others. The essential aim of clinical supervision should be to increase the resilience of the professional, ensuring they can act on risk appropriately as well as guaranteeing and improving the quality of care or intervention they are delivering (Wallbank &

Woods, 2012). The assumption that 'supervision' is a uniform experience, despite the variety of contexts it is practised in, impacts the ability of those practising it to understand its essential aims.

What are the different types of supervision and what do they entail?

As we have outlined, the intended function or purpose of supervision will impact how it is delivered and which skills are needed to deliver it effectively. Kadushin (1992) defined three main functions of supervision: educational, managerial and supportive. Proctor (1986) has a similar view of the key functions of supervision, although her terminology is different; she refers to the normative, formative and restorative aspects of supervision. We will review the key functions and the differences between them. The most important point is that you understand what outcome you want your supervision to achieve and therefore what function you need to be using. You can use a mixture of functions during one supervision session.

Educational/formative

This type of supervision is directed towards the educational development of the practitioner and the fulfilment of potential. The supervisee is considered lesser in experience and understanding than the supervisor. The primary aim within educational supervision is for the supervisee to learn from the supervisor through observation, reflection and exploration of their work. The measure of supervision success is an increase in the knowledge, attitude and skills required by the individual to carry out their role.

All clinical supervision could be described as an experiential learning experience because supervisors and supervisees are sharing perspectives in order to think differently and develop the individual's practice. What is different about conducting supervision with specific educational outcomes is the power differential: the experienced supervisor is teaching and testing the less experienced supervisee. The supervisee is often reliant on passing a subjective marker in order to meet requirements and the supervision space is therefore filled with expectations and hidden aspects of the self. 'Students' are likely to share information about their performance that demonstrates their capability. The skill of the supervisor lies in providing a comfortable enough space for the supervisee to be able to reveal those parts of their performance that are less capable or problematic.

The supervisor's role is to provide feedback or direction for the supervisee, helping them to become an increasingly competent practitioner. Supervision is usually based around the content of the work, with opportunities to reflect with the student about the work itself. Observations and working alongside the supervisor are common methods, and the success of the supervision is usually measured by demonstrations of increased knowledge, skills and understanding against baseline measures, such as a student contract or appraisal system.

Administrative/managerial/normative

Within this type of supervision, the relationship is focused on performance, the promotion and maintenance of quality standards, adherence to policies and good practice. This is the quality assurance dimension of supervision. As with educational/formative functions, all types of supervision will have a normative and administrative aspect to them, ensuring that the practice being discussed within the supervisory space is adhering to standards. Record-keeping and noting attendance, content of the discussions or agreed actions and outcomes are all administrative duties. The difference when conducting managerial supervision is that the discussions are usually explicit about the measurement of performance against a target or goal.

The managerial aspect of the supervisor's role will be clear where a line management relationship exists, but can also be implicit where the supervisor is more senior than the supervisee. Supervisees will think differently about a supervisor who is in a more senior position within their professional role, to how they would think about a peer or someone more junior to them. Considering the boundaries of the relationships in supervision is important, as if the supervisor accepts responsibility for the adherence of the supervisee to the professional and ethical standards of the organisation and job role, then the role becomes a managerial one. The supervisee is expected to operate within codes, laws and norms and the predominant use of supervision time is the measurement of performance against these standards. The space becomes one where the supervisee demonstrates their compliance as well as their competence.

Supportive/restorative

This function of supervision contains elements of psychological support including listening, supporting and challenging the supervisee to improve their capacity to cope, especially in managing difficult and stressful situations. The writing around the supportive and restorative functions of supervision tends to refer to these as inadvertent benefits of supervision, rather than its primary function or purpose. Commonly, organisational supervision focuses on the content of someone's workload, for example specific patients or families, and this is considered the most important reflective aspect of the supervision, rather than the professional and their well-being. In this approach to supervision, any supportive or restorative function is often simply a result of the professional feeling better about the content of their work.

Supportive functions of supervision can also be found in less formal supervision environments. The support that colleagues give to each other, supporting morale and job satisfaction just by sharing their experiences, is a good example. There is a common misunderstanding that undertaking any type of clinical supervision will provide a restorative experience. It is important to note that clinical supervision in itself has not been established as restorative, especially if it does not include any restorative elements. For example, a supervisee who experiences educational supervision and finds their work performance below par may not find that the session leaves them feeling restored unless the supervisor provides a restorative element as part of the session.

The next chapter will review the evidence for the effectiveness of restorative resilience supervision. The difference between this model of supervision and the educational and managerial functions of supervision is its emphasis on the individual. It is not the work product that comes under scrutiny, but rather the individual undertaking the work and the impact that the work is having on them.

A note about power

It is important to note the power differential between two people within clinical supervision. The role and responsibilities of the supervisor can be different depending on their professional role. If a supervisor is also the individual's manager or has managerial responsibilities for them, this will change the dynamic of the session. Additionally, having a supervisor who is not the individual's line manager has been shown to be key to achieving a successful supervisor/supervisee relationship (Cutcliffe & Hyrkäs, 2006).Conversely, if an individual is being supervised by someone outside of their immediate profession or someone who is junior to them, then the information they reveal to their supervisor may have a different meaning.

The usefulness of the session comes from the power difference between the supervisor and supervisee being open and discussed. If the supervisor has responsibility for the work product of the supervisee, then the session will always have a managerial tone to it. If there is no such relationship, then this needs to be made clear and a plan needs to be made for dealing with any difficulties that might arise. The experience of supervision with another can create an artificial state of anxiety for the professional. This is because they may feel examined or critiqued. Being aware of the power balance in the session will ensure that the professional can develop their relationship with their supervisor and reveal their honest state rather than an artificial one.

Type of delivery?

There are a number of different ways of completing clinical supervision: individual, closed group sessions (invited members only), open group sessions (where invitation is extended to everyone), peer networks (professionally based, where groups of practitioners support each other), online supervision, Skype sessions and active sessions (where exercise or activities are included as part of the session). The way in which a supervisor chooses to deliver the supervision should be based around the objectives of the sessions and the individual supervisee's needs. Each different type of delivery will require a different skillset and it is therefore important for supervisors to consider whether they or the organisation have those skills in place.

To ensure a robust supervision strategy, the organisation needs to be clear on the approach it is taking to supervision and the objectives that it wants to achieve. The model of supervision needs to be explicit, so that the supervision activity can be measured against its objectives.

Why supervision supports resilience

The literature around resilience and stress consistently refers to the social support networks that individuals surround themselves with. When we enter a 'stressed' mode we are less able to contribute to positive relationships around us, and ensuring that we have supportive relationships is important. Having a close positive bond with at least one other person is the most significant mediator of stress, with affection from members of extended family being a commonly cited resilience builder. Professionally, having a strong relationship with a supervisor and finding a safe place to explore difficulties is highly protective.

Given that it takes time to initiate and maintain friendships/relationships, the professional who gives their all to their work life is limiting their resilience on two counts. First, the work is more likely to be a stressor and to cause burnout; second, the professional is unable to rely on their support network, as they have neglected to invest the time needed to build strong bonds. Utilising a supervisory model that focuses on the individual and their resilience factors means that they can build the supportive foundations around them, not just explore their work content.

For the individual, being able to express their needs to those around them is a key protective factor in building resilience. Supervisees need to be able to tell people what they are capable of and what is too much, as well as having the capacity to negotiate when things become overwhelming. This means that people need to have confidence in themselves as individuals, in order to express sometimes negative emotions towards others in a way that enables the relationship to continue. If professionals can model this and begin to express their needs within a supervisory space, this is a great start to implementing it within their workplace.

The capacity that individuals have to demonstrate self-efficacy or the ability to produce a desired result or outcome is also a significant resilience builder. If the individual believes that they have the power and control to determine what happens to them, then they are less likely to be impacted by events. This is also linked to self-esteem and confidence levels – the more positive people are about themselves, the less likely they are to be impacted by external events. Within the supervisory space, the individual's supervisor can explore their positive aspects and not just focus on what they are not doing.

Earlier we discussed the personality factors that can support or hinder individuals' capacity to manage stressors. The capacity for professionals to develop self-monitoring skills is important for them in noticing when they start to feel under pressure. For the individual, being able to demonstrate self-control at times when they feel unable to cope with the demands being placed on them is a significant skill in enabling them to demonstrate boundaried behaviour. Significant features of good supervision include letting the individual know when their behaviour changes and supporting them to identify triggers as well as how to reverse the impact.

As we have explored, the role of the helper means that they are available to others and prone to want to make things better. This makes it difficult for the individual to operate in a boundaried way; often they will opt to say yes to all that is asked of them. The supervision space can explore current job demands and how the professional responds to further requests for more. This builds resilience but also supports the professional to recognise how they are exacerbating their own difficulties.

Unclear or conflicted expectations are also a factor in an individual behaving in an unboundaried manner. This is a common feature of working in a multidisciplinary team, but the professional needs to have the presence of mind to constantly re-negotiate their role in relation to the wider team. Working in a hostile or defensive atmosphere also increases vulnerability. We know that difficult behaviours increase as stress rises, so people are more likely to experience a challenging environment where demands are high. Creating a space through supervision where the environment, and the individual's reaction to the environment, can be discussed is also useful for building resilience.

Working in an unethical environment is a further risk to vulnerability. Individuals tend to be drawn to helping and caring work because of their personal values, and a context that does not support this will compromise them. Supervision enables the individual to reflect on their value system and make attempts to change their working environment to align the two. Ultimately, if the two cannot be aligned, it may drive them to move to another role that is a better fit.

Finally, a lack of communication increases risk. This is often a result of the pace of change meaning the level of communication cannot not keep up. Supervision enables individuals to reflect on the realities of working in a fast-paced environment and how they can contribute and feed back to their line manager and others to ensure that the right communication is received in a timely way. This avoids getting into conflict situations about the lack of communication or spending precious time complaining about a situation that they are not able to change.

Chapter 7:
Why restorative resilience supervision?

We will now focus on the specific model of restorative resilience supervision. We will explore its origins as well as its use within the helping professions before moving on to look at the elements of the model itself.

The development of the restorative resilience approach came in response to an original piece of research undertaken by the author which looked at how nurses, doctors and midwives responded to miscarriage, stillbirth and loss experienced as part of their work (Wallbank & Robertson, 2008). The idea for this research arose from time spent with families who were experiencing negative psychological responses from their birth experiences. During the retelling of their birth stories, families would describe the involvement of the staff members who featured strongly both in mitigating and exacerbating the impact of what had happened. The emotive impact on the families was clear. Less well explored was how the events and the emotions of the families had impacted on the professionals.

The author's personal experience also impacted this thinking. Having a parent working on a high dependency cardiac unit, dealing with death and loss most days, showed that the emotional toll of the work was often observed by close family members and friends of the professional, but not necessarily acknowledged by their organisation. The details of patient care were not shared within the family because of the sensitive nature of the work, but the impact was clearly significant.

The original research used quantitative measures[1] of stress, burnout and compassion satisfaction (the pleasure gained from a job) to determine how professionals processed their experiences of loss. The measures showed that in two large hospital trusts the experience of caring for a family experiencing loss evoked negative reactions for staff (Wallbank & Robertson, 2008). Feeling distressed or overwhelmed could be seen as a normal part of this work, however the negative impact of the stress experience created adverse effects within the staff members. These reactions manifested as significant and clinical levels of subjective stress – that is, stress episodes linked to these experiences. While there were existing structures in place to support staff via occupational health and specialist counselling midwives, these remained largely under-utilised.

---

1   Professional Quality of Life Scale (ProQOL) (Stamm, 2008); Impact of Events Scale (IES) (Horowitz, 1982); Positive and Negative Affect Schedule (PANAS) (Watson *et al*, 1988)

The experience of undertaking the research itself was also a significant indicator of the distress that professionals were experiencing. The data for the project was returned by professionals in less than three weeks, which is highly unusual for this type of research and suggested that the author was asking questions that the professionals were keen to answer. While promoting the study, the author was approached by staff members who were distressed and wanting to share their experiences.

The research took place within an environment that was not regarded as particularly stressful or emotive, perhaps, as mentioned earlier, because the delivery of new life is seen as happy and positive work. This meant that the staff involved in the research were more vulnerable to stress. It was not expected of their workplace to acknowledge the negative emotional impact of their work. Other than the usual support systems, which did not appear to be accessed by the staff, the professionals were not offered an opportunity to process their workplace experiences unless a catastrophic or traumatic event – for example, a mother's death – occurred.

Developing an intervention

Rather than just leave it to others to answer questions about what should be done with an identified problem, or professionals feeling under pressure and overwhelmed, the author decided to design and test a potential solution for reducing the impact of the work via clinical supervision. Having researched the various models of supervision, it was clear that although there was limited evidence of a restorative value to clinical supervision, a bespoke model would need to be developed. This model needed to enable staff to process their workplace experiences and to feel less overwhelmed by them. It also needed to enable the staff to learn more about how they could avoid becoming overwhelmed in the future and to develop protective coping techniques.

As previously mentioned, there was little research that explored the efficacy of clinical supervision, especially in reducing stress and burnout, so it was important to design and deliver an intervention in a way that would begin to develop a quantitative evidence base. While there was a myriad of evidence that discussed the emotive nature of helping work, solutions and recommendations tended to be offered as a result of individual case studies. They were not grounded in evidence and tended to be a reflection of the preferences of the particular authors.

The first pilot study began in 2009 and was designed as a small randomised controlled study. The author took two groups of midwives, doctors and nurses and randomly assigned them to either the 'clinical supervision training group' or the 'no intervention group'. Within the study, the psychologist's role was to deliver the new model of clinical supervision and to train the staff, both formally and through the experience of receiving the supervision, to be able to deliver it to others.

The only activity that the non-intervention group undertook was to have their stress, burnout and compassion satisfaction levels measured before and at the end of the study. The measures used were similar to those of the initial study, as this provided a large set of international data we could measure the results against.

The intervention group undertook a training day and six sessions of the model of clinical supervision now called 'restorative supervision.' They also had their burnout, compassion satisfaction and stress levels measured before and at the end of the intervention.

Results for the treatment group showed significant differences in subjective stress (t (15) = 6.59, p = .000) with average scores decreased from 29 to seven; compassion satisfaction scores (t (15) = 2.66, p = .001) with average scores increased from 37 to 41; burnout (associated with feelings of hopelessness and difficulties in dealing with work) (t (15) = 6.70, p = .000) with average scores decreased from 27 to 14; and compassion fatigue (related to secondary exposure to stressful events) (t (15) = 2.18, p = .004) with average scores decreased from 16 to 12. Post-study results showed no statistically significant difference in the scores of the control group compared with their earlier scores.

We learned from the original study that a systematic, individual and restorative approach to clinical supervision appeared to have a positive impact on the reduction of stress for staff working in obstetrics and gynaecology. The results were not limited to the quantitative elements alone; there were observable physical changes that the staff underwent as they started to be able to focus more on their own needs. Anecdotally, the participants reported feeling that they were required to cope with workplace events as part of their professional role, and that they experienced an inability to express themselves to significant others and a sense of responsibility not to burden colleagues with their experiences. The events that the participants experienced at work appeared to significantly impact their ability to think and make decisions. This finding was ubiquitous across the group.

The capacity of the supervision intervention to normalise the emotional demands and subsequent effects that the professionals were experiencing seemed significant in its effectiveness. At this early stage there was already recognition of the parallel relationship between the carer feeling their best and the quality of care they delivered.

Further testing

Further research was then undertaken with large groups of community nurses, doctors and social workers, and this time the psychologist trained a number of supervisors to undertake both the teaching elements and the direct delivery of the programme of supervision. The supervisors were of average grade and job experience and had an interest in supervision. This was considered important for sustainability and to demonstrate that this model could be taught and delivered by others. It also showed that the results were not directly attributable to the mental health expertise of the psychologist but could also be delivered within a peer group environment.

Before the training day, participants were given information about the restorative approach and the evaluation elements of the supervision to allow them to give consent to their participation. During the training day they were asked to complete a baseline questionnaire, which was completed again at the end of the sixth session. The results showed that the model was again successful in maintaining compassion satisfaction, even suggesting a slight increase in this area. On average, burnout was reduced by 43% and stress by 62%. This meant a calmer workforce who were able to think more clearly.

The programme continues to be delivered to a range of professionals across public and private sector organisations in the UK, Ireland and Australia. This includes work with:

- acute nurses
- community children's nurses
- designated child protection doctors and nurses
- named child protection nurses
- obstetricians
- health visitors
- school nurses
- midwives
- managers and supervisors of all levels
- hospice workers
- early years teams
- social workers.

At the time of writing over 5,000 individuals have been trained in the programme and evaluated using the measures developed within the initial study. Based on these results, we have found:

The ProQOL data shows us that the average score for compassion satisfaction is 37 (SD=7; alpha scale reliability=0.87). About 25% of people score higher than 42 and about 25% of people score below 33. Participants undertaking the programme on average score 43.20 (SD 4.48) at baseline, improving to 45.12 (SD 3.87) after they undertake the programme. The higher compassion satisfaction is, the more pleasure someone is gaining from their role.

The average score on the burnout scale is 22 (SD=6.0; alpha scale reliability=0.72). About 25% of people score above 27 and about 25% of people score below 18 (Stamm, 2008). Participants at baseline score on average 43.94 (SD 3.98) and this improves to 25.71 (4.23), which shows significant reductions in burnout.

The impact of events (IES) measure can be also used to identify levels of stress, with 22 or less being considered low, 23–31 being average, and 31 and above being regarded as high (Horowitz, 1982). At baseline, the research undertaken by the author showed stress levels were at 43.96 (SD 4.19) and, alongside the burnout levels of helpers, should be concerning for organisations. Post supervision, the IES scores reduce to 19.81 (SD 5.21) showing a significant reduction in stress.

Qualitative feedback

Themes have developed across the cohorts of participants undertaking the programme, which tend to be strikingly similar regardless of professional role or work context and are also supported by the stress and coping literature.

Staff undertaking this type of supervision described higher levels of job satisfaction. We know that being satisfied with your role and gaining pleasure from your work is protective against stress, and this was considered a significant and positive finding. Staff also reported being more able to provide compassionate care; they felt more in tune with those they were helping or caring for, and therefore reported that the experience was more positive for the individuals receiving care as well as providing it.

Professionals were less likely to have time off sick and could therefore provide continuity of care or helping, which meant that the pressure within teams was also reduced, as staff were required to pick up their colleagues' work less often.

Inappropriate workplace behaviours were being gently challenged and moved forwards within teams rather than needlessly burdening management. As teams became more functional, they were able to process and deal with these difficulties themselves. This was especially the case where all members of the team were undertaking the programme.

The way in which individuals identified and worked collaboratively with both their employers and those outside of their organisations was described as improved. Professionals were more likely to raise their hands and volunteer for additional tasks, but in a boundaried way rather than because no one else was volunteering. They appeared to be able to recognise the strengths within the system rather than just critiquing it and this reduced their sense of vulnerability.

Professionals' health behaviours also improved. Whether it be smoking, eating or sleeping, professionals were driven to make better choices as they were more able to focus on themselves. Overall, the research observed a calmer workforce and staff members who had space to think.

Professionals themselves commented:

> '*Restorative supervision came at a time when the workload was phenomenal and this provided a secure place to offload. I had a lot of issues about feeling valued by the Trust and although they have not been resolved, it gave me the opportunity for containment.*'

> '*I have found restorative supervision very helpful; it is a unique space and opportunity to talk freely about the issues affecting the way I work. I really value my sessions and always come out of them feeling calmer, more positive and focused than when I went in.*'

> '*I have found restorative supervision really useful. I was a complete novice to supervision at the start, and found the sessions a little daunting as I wasn't used to talking about myself. However, I have now managed to relax during the sessions, and have learnt a lot about myself and have found this has helped me in my practice.*'

> '*I have found the planned time for [restorative] supervision invaluable to my practice. I feel valued and rejuvenated as an employee after the session so therefore the clients I am dealing with are getting a better service.*'

Development of a longer-term group approach

The final stage of development was to ensure that individuals who had benefited from the individual sessions and were in a more resilient mindset could continue to maintain this. A sustainable model of implementation was developed for organisations that were not able to continue to invest in individual sessions.

Following the initial six sessions, professionals were then brought together into groups of five. A further piece of research (Wallbank, 2013) showed that this approach was successful over time in maintaining and continuing to improve compassion satisfaction, stress and burnout through the process of the group supervision.

This meant that organisations could continue to maintain the programme once the initial training had been completed, and had confidence with the group supervision sessions to support professionals in managing the emotional demands of their role.

The restorative groups continued to foster teamwork and also had inadvertent positive benefits in workplace functioning. By experiencing the highs and lows of the workplace within small groups, these could be explored as a team and the wider functioning of the professional teams as a result improved further.

What does the research mean?

What we feel able to say following the research and working with large groups of professionals is that this model seems to work. Individuals find it useful in supporting them to process their workplace experiences and it restores their capacity to think clearly. It will not replace all forms of supervision that may be used within the workplace, however the restorative emphasis is useful in building the resilience of the individual and this means that they retain their capacity to think, are able to demonstrate effective helping work and appropriate governance, and remain open to learning. If we start with the restorative resilience approach as a foundation or springboard for maintaining the capacity to think and act in a consistent way, then the professional is more able to manage their daily pressure.

Chapter 8:
Key elements of the restorative resilience model

This chapter discusses how the principles of the restorative resilience model work as well as the key skills that are used in creating a highly effective supervisory space.

Principles

We begin with the important principles of the model. The first principle of restorative resilience supervision is that the focus is on the person, not the case or individual patient/family/person that they happen to be helping or caring for. This is to ensure that the process of restoring the individual professional is sustainable. If we restore the capacity of the individual to think clearly then they can apply new energy to all of their work, not just the one aspect of it that happened to be the priority on that day.

Next, we must ensure that the time spent in supervision is effective, not just for the individual supervisee but for the supervisor and the organisation. We do this by ensuring that the goals for the supervision are aligned with the organisation and individual, and that we constantly review and negotiate the agenda. Organisations may often overlook this, as an assumption is made that all supervision is effective. Organisations also often neglect to measure the effectiveness of the sessions. The restorative resilience training provides an evaluation tool to enable organisations to have confidence that it continues to be useful.

We then consider the structures that surround the professional and consider how the supervision sessions will support those structures. We know that a supported professional is the most effective, so we want to create feedback mechanisms within and outside of the organisation to facilitate an effective work environment. The relationship between individuals and the system they work in is key to their success and we want to foster a productive relationship.

Finally, we want to ensure that a safe environment is created for us to consider how poor behaviour is challenged. If we think back to the chapter dealing with stress (Chapter 5), and what we know about behaviours under stress, we can consider what types of behaviour such as distress, anger or lateness might be attributed stress. An important aspect of this is for the supervisor and supervisee to work together to understand what is acceptable behaviour and what makes stress conditions worse.

It is unusual that a professional is able to hold a mirror up to their own personal characteristics and explore how these are impacting on the demands of their role. Exploring this knowledge in a safe way with the supervisor enables professionals to understand what they are themselves contributing to a problem, which parts of the problem are not theirs to own and how they can take action going forward.

Foundation skills

The model of restorative resilience supervision draws on six key skills:

- Emotional containment.
- Reflective practice.
- Stress inoculation.
- Resilience training.
- Action learning.
- Foundation coaching.

Precisely when to intervene using each of these skills will depend upon where the supervisee is in terms of their own resilience and their capacity to think.

The work performance zones

Delivering supervision to a large number of professionals has shown us that the cognitive (thinking) approach and psychological state of the supervisee both influence their needs in supervision. The model uses 'zones' to describe the predominant states that supervisees seem to come into supervision with, and then uses the skills above to support supervisees in these zones. This is not to suggest that the professional stays in one zone all the time, but that the amount of time they spend there influences their overall productivity. These zones are illustrated in Figure 8.1.

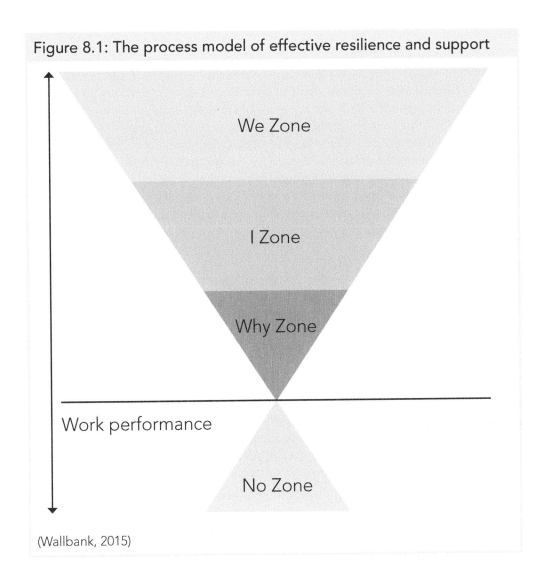

Figure 8.1: The process model of effective resilience and support

We Zone

I Zone

Why Zone

Work performance

No Zone

(Wallbank, 2015)

No Zone

A professional who spends the majority of their time in the No Zone is usually one who is suffering the adverse effects of stress. They can be unnecessarily difficult or disruptive, or completely withdrawn/disengaged from the work environment. If we look again at the chapter on stress (Chapter 5), we can see that professionals use both these strategies – becoming disruptive or becoming withdrawn – to help them cope. What the professional will often not consider, however, is the impact they have on others. By not wanting to engage or participate they are usually saying no to all requests, regardless of how reasonable these may be, and others around them may subsequently pick up additional roles. Productivity for the individual in this zone is low.

The energy levels of professionals in the No Zone are usually low and you will recognise them as being quite difficult to sit with or talk to; often they feel slowed down or just difficult. They are more likely to describe conflicts with others, whether this be other professionals, managers or the people they are working with. They are also likely to be more emotional, and this can be a range of emotions. It is not the emotions that are exclusive to those in this group, but rather the intensity of them and the hopelessness that seems to accompany them. Professionals in this zone are less likely to derive a sense of pleasure from their work and will be openly negative about their environment and work content.

Why Zone

This zone describes another more negative experience, but one which is a step up from the No Zone. These professionals are anxious and operate in a mode in which they question everything. This is not done in order to gain useful information or seek clarification, but is the result of the individual having a nervous or fearful energy. There is often too much on their mind. Productivity is negative or neutral at best in this zone.

Professionals in the Why Zone are often consumed with an event/events that have taken place in the workplace. It could be a team dispute, difficult work experience where things did not go to plan, conflict or lack of progression. The important thing to bear in mind is that we will all experience being in this zone at some point. Our thinking skills are not great in this zone as we give all of our cognitive efforts to focusing on previous events which we are unable to change.

Both the No and Why zones require emotional containment, good listening skills and reflection to move professionals into a more positive place. Action learning sets and stress inoculation/resilience building (key tools to build on individuals' usual coping and areas of strength) ensure they do not return to these zones without strategies for exiting. It is the sense of being 'stuck' in the zone that becomes problematic. Functional professionals who learn skills to exit the areas still visit these zones but can equally leave them. The specific skills will be looked at in more detail later.

I Zone

This is an energetic zone and tends to increase productivity. The professional is able to focus more on what they need to do to enhance their learning, practice, or overall health and well-being. The talk in this zone is about what 'I' can do to learn, change or move their situation. The professional recognises their own behaviour and contribution to events or situations. They are thinking and expressing themselves clearly.

We Zone

This is again a high energy area. The professional is creative and energetic, thinking of new ideas to benefit themselves, clients/patients and organisations. They are a pleasure to work around and you are energised by being with them. The discussions tend to be about the supervisee and others, and the supervisee tends to be looking forwards as well as outwards from their own job role and organisation.

In these zones, supervision with individuals utilises coaching and action learning interventions to reflect back to the supervisee the content of the conversations and what their positive triggers seem to be so that they can begin to recognise this in themselves. This will help them identify what can interfere with their effectiveness, how they can support their own learning and growth, and what the risk factors relating to their work area or project are.

What are the skills needed?

The restorative resilience supervision programme was designed and developed to use a mixture of experiential learning and exposure to the model itself. The use of each specific skill listed on p64 builds as the supervisor becomes more proficient and has opportunities to practice. There is no hard and fast rule about how individuals move through the zones; they can move in and out during the session depending upon the topic of discussion. The key skill in applying the model is being able to assess where the supervisee is at that time.

Moving from the No and Why Zones

Using emotional containment

The skills of emotional containment are important in enabling the supervisor to recognise and support the professional to process their anxiety/fear or negative emotions relating to their work. Being able to identify triggers, process emotions and move into thinking about positive coping strategies are all key skills for the professional. Emotional containment is not just for use when you want to support someone in an unhelpful place, but is the most useful method of drawing someone into a more useful way of thinking.

The supervisor uses basic counselling skills to support the person, such as open-ended questions, affirmative answers (validating, supportive), and reflecting with the individual on why they may be feeling or thinking the way they are.

The supervisor also becomes skilled in recognising the impact that the supervision environment has on the professional's capacity to think and ensuring that they provide an appropriate space for maximum effectiveness of the sessions.

Through their experiential learning and the supervision sessions that the supervisors receive themselves, they become more aware of their own contributions to the sessions, how the power dynamic works between the supervisor and supervisee, and how to work with silence. They will work on their own body language and perhaps unconscious communications, so that these become more effective and not a distraction in the sessions. The key to emotional containment is also understanding how to boundary both the session itself and the interventions that the supervisor makes.

The No Zone and the Why Zone tend to be experienced by individuals when they are anxious, fearful or negative about their work. They remain in these zones exhibiting this behaviour as an expression of those negative worries and concerns, and by behaving in this way it helps them to feel less anxious or fearful, but they remain stuck. By emotionally containing their concerns and helping them to move to a more productive thinking style, this reduces their anxiety and they feel able to move out of this zone of thinking and feeling.

Reflective practice

Within this model the supervisor uses reflective practice to link patterns of behaviour and thinking styles so that the supervisee can learn from those actions, feelings and behaviours. These may not just relate to actual clinical or care practice but to everyday issues in working with a team and others. By facilitating the supervisee to describe situations in detail, the supervisor gains an in-depth understanding of the events. The supervisor and supervisee work together to identify patterns of behaviour and dominant thinking and/or feeling patterns. The session is then used to agree what will be taken away and worked on.

The combination of these techniques supports the professional to develop more helpful ways of thinking and coping with their current situation and enables them to begin to think more clearly.

There are a number of models of reflective practice and action learning that supervisors can draw upon to support professionals within their sessions. As we described earlier, the purpose of reflective practice in this model is the linking of patterns to enable learning to take place about thoughts, feelings and behaviours. These may not just relate to actual clinical or care practice but everyday issues working with a team and others. The reflective experience needs to be followed by action learning to ensure that the learning is developed.

Let's take the example of a professional who finds herself overwhelmed by her workload. Rather than being in a situation where she is controlling what she takes on and commits to, she is always volunteering for additional work. Exploring the last time this happened, what she was thinking, feeling and what she subsequently did can be a useful way to understand the behaviour. In this example, the professional feels guilty in her team meeting that no one is volunteering for the work; despite being at capacity, she raises her hand to take on the work. Seeing that she may have capacity, later in the day her manager asks her to do something else and she agrees without explaining to her manager how busy she is. The professional does not feel able to communicate constructively about her workload and therefore what her priorities should be. She tends to feel helpless and guilty and this keeps her in a vicious circle.

We want to use the learning from reflective practice to plan for future events so that this knowledge is put into practice. This is what sets it apart from just having a containing experience and listening actively to the story. Once the supervisor and supervisee have made the links and agreed what could be contributing to the session, you then enter a change mode.

The core skills to enable a supervisor to facilitate reflective practice are similar to those of emotional containment: active listening, reflecting and asking questions to clarify. You can use reflection before the action itself, if, for example, the supervisee is concerned about an event that is coming up and the last time they were in a similar situation things did not go to plan. You can use role play to practice what they might do 'during the action', as it teaches the supervisee the skill of reflection while they are engaged in an activity. You want to encourage an explicit discussion of what they might say and do in order to get the supervisee to really think about their motivations and intentions. After action tends to be the preferred method of reflective practice i.e. describing the event after they have experienced it.

One of the key skills a supervisor must master is the ability to test out perspectives during reflective practice. A number of factors can impact the accuracy of our memory, not least of which is the emotionality of the event (Lacy & Stark, 2013). Actively listening to an account means testing, challenging and clarifying the information in order to understand it better. Asking the supervisee what others who were present may have said, what others have said since the event and what their views might be now is a powerful way of adding depth to their reflections. We know that the process of retelling a story and sharing experiences impacts the memory of the events and subsequent psychological responses (Paterson *et al*, 2015).

Figure 8.2: Restorative resilience reflective practice model demonstrates the cycle the supervisee is entering into in order to achieve behaviour change.

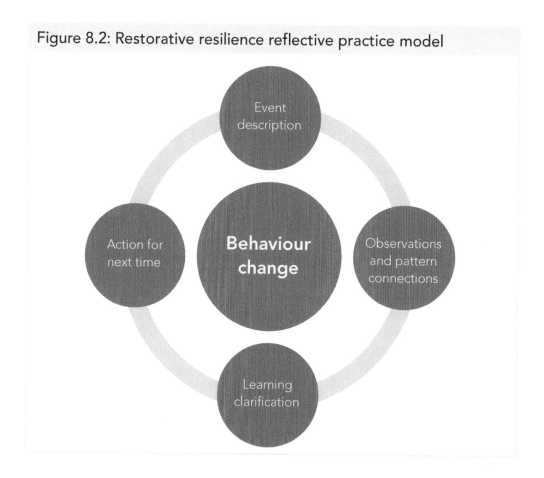

Figure 8.2: Restorative resilience reflective practice model

Remaining with the I Zone

Stress inoculation

In order to ensure that the professional is able to remain resilient and move themselves out of the more negative zones, the supervisor needs to spend some of the session thinking with the professional about stress inoculation. This begins with the supervisor sharing their knowledge of stress. This is useful as we have found that professionals with a raised awareness of what stress is, what the causes are and the protective factors, are much more able to consider their own responses to situations. This also supports the supervisor and supervisee to identify any stress habits that are already in place.

By working through the supervisee's key stressors, the supervisor is able to identify which stressors are not going to change and therefore need to be accepted, and how they want to work with the stressors that can be reduced. This may be by changing how a supervisee thinks about a stressor or taking affirmative action such as factoring in travel time to feel less time pressured. Agreeing an action plan with the supervisee is key to ensuring that the session is effective and the supervisee remains accountable. The main objective for the stress inoculation is ensuring that the professional's response to a stressor is deliberate and considered, rather than automatic.

In order to achieve this, the supervisor and supervisee first work together to identify the key stressors. This is not just accepting the first response – for example, 'My workload is overwhelming,' – but exploring what, specifically, is the problem or trigger.

The supervisor will work with the supervisee in a holistic way, drawing on and helping them recognise their strengths in their wider life rather than just those strengths related to their work. The space will then be used to consider unrealistic and negative beliefs about the stressor that the supervisee may have. This can take a number of sessions, especially if the supervisee believes that everything is beyond their control. The aim is to open up the thinking of the supervisee about what they can bring to the problem.

Finally, the supervisor will support the supervisee in developing assertion and negotiation skills, specifically, the following.

Assertion:

- Being open in expressing wishes, thoughts and feelings, and encouraging others to do likewise.
- Listening to the views of others and responding appropriately, whether in agreement with those views or not.
- Accepting responsibilities and being able to delegate to others.
- Regularly expressing appreciation of others for what they have done or are doing.
- Being able to admit to mistakes and apologise.
- Maintaining self-control.
- Behaving as an equal to others.

Negotiation:

- Preparation.
- Discussion.
- Clarification of goals.
- Negotiating towards a win-win outcome.

This process, from identifying the stressor to developing assertion and negotiation skills, is shown in **Figure 8.3**, which can be used as a tool to work through with your supervisee so that they are able to see clearly each step of the process.

Figure 8.3: Stress inoculation for use within restorative resilience

Stress inoculation
Improving your ability to thrive in a stressful environment
1   Identify the stressor
2   Maximise strengths ■ Lifestyle ■ Health ■ Well-being ■ How are you functioning?
3   Using supervision space to challenge negative and unrealistic beliefs
4   Working together with problem solving techniques
5   Teaching assertive and negotiation skills

Resilience training

Staying in the I Zone means retaining the capacity to reflect on what you need as an individual to function well within your role. The idea of resilience training builds on stress inoculation by getting the supervisee to think about their internal and external resources. Using a mental inventory of what resilience looks like and possible skills they are lacking, the supervisor reviews with the supervisee their overall functioning. Elements such as lifestyle, health and well-being are considered, as well as their daily functioning. The supervisor's role is to work with the supervisee to solve problems. They use the assertive and negotiation skills to improve the supervisee's ability to deal with strong feelings, and increase their capacity to cope as well as to identify procrastination.

The supervisor then works with the supervisee to consider their protective factors. This process begins by looking at internal, personal strengths. These are feelings, attitudes and beliefs within the professional, and the challenge for the supervisee is to identify those elements of themselves that they feel are positive and strong or which benefit their work. We know that professionals who have pride in themselves tend to behave with an appropriate level of autonomy and are significantly more trusted in their work.

Linking back to the stress inoculation work, the supervisor will then help the professional to look at what skills they have at their disposal. The capacity to communicate openly and honestly, ensuring that they are able to get their message across is a start, but it is also important that they have the capacity to listen and reconcile differences and are able to understand and act on the results of the communication. The capacity of the professional to recognise their own and others' feelings, and express them through words and behaviours that do not violate the feelings and rights of others, is a critical element of communication. This is a crucial skill, especially in highly emotive workplaces.

The capacity of the professional to solve problems by utilising the resources around them is also a key skill. The resilient professional is able to negotiate solutions with others and may find alternative solutions. The persistence to stay with an issue until it is resolved is a further developed skill.

Finally, the supervisor will consider areas of deficit that need work and how to support the supervisee in building trusting relationships with others around them to ensure they are supported moving forward.

Only when the professional is in the We Zone

It is important that the coaching element of the restorative supervision model is not introduced until supervisees are restored and focusing beyond themselves.

Foundation coaching

The objective of the foundation coaching is to identify with the supervisee where they want to be or what they want to achieve in order to move forward. This may be something they want to achieve or change personally or that is related to the impact of their work. Finding out the supervisee's future plans and comparing this to the reality of their current situation illuminates the gaps between where they are and where they want to be. The supervisor's role is to support the supervisee to develop an action plan to reduce or overcome the gaps.

Supervisors usually work with foundation coaching when an individual is at their best – energetic and creative and therefore able to benefit from this style of working. This usually occurs towards the end of the six individual sessions, but may even be possible from the first session if the individual being supervised is already in a strong emotional place.

Chapter 9:
Case studies

The following chapter presents three case studies that illustrate restorative resilience supervision skills in practice.

Case study 1: Sandra, community nurse and educational lead

Sandra is an experienced community nurse who works with children under five and their families. Her role also requires her to be the education lead and to perform a range of other nursing and support roles across the teams in her service. This is a split role which has evolved over time and therefore has no clear time allocation for each role. The roles used to be undertaken by full-time staff. Sandra's stress and burnout levels are high, but most concerning is the fact that her compassion satisfaction is very low.

No Zone behaviours

Sandra arrived for a restorative resilience session exhibiting some difficult behaviours. She had her arms crossed for most of the session and shared lots of eye-rolling and muttering. The group being supervised with Sandra appeared used to these behaviours as they separated themselves from her physically and she spent the session not connecting with the group. When the supervisor talked to her afterwards, she became extremely distressed and began to describe some of the pressures on her. The supervisor made it clear to Sandra that she wanted to support her with these difficulties and that the first step was to enable her to understand the stress reaction she was experiencing. This encouraged Sandra to participate further in the next session.

Learning point: Supervisors need to feel equipped to understand and manage these behaviours, so they do not respond inappropriately because they are feeling personally attacked.

Why Zone

The sessions with Sandra began by focusing on where she was finding pleasure in her work. This was important as Sandra was experiencing high levels of hopelessness and feelings that nothing could be changed. Sandra was fixated by events of the last five years and the fact that there used to be so many more staff members. She could name all of them and their job roles. The supervisor focused with Sandra on the time before the changes, in order to learn what a more resilient and happy Sandra looked like. Sandra's confidence in her organisation was low and she was immersed with concern that she would be the next one 'targeted' for redundancy. The behaviours she was demonstrating seemed to be communicating: 'If you do not care for me, why should I care for you?'

The culture within the organisation seemed to be one of distrust, questioning and scrutinising everything, perhaps beyond the appropriate focus one should expect in a public sector organisation. The supervisor's role was to personalise the experience with Sandra, helping her to see this as less of an organisation-wide response, and enable her to consider who was having a positive and negative impact on her within the organisation.

Throughout the sessions the supervisor used mirroring skills to reflect back what Sandra was saying and her physical presentation. Teaching her to calm down her breathing and relax under discussion was key to being able to communicate her points clearly. The supervisor was then able to provide a challenge to some of Sandra's more assumptive thinking – for example, 'They all hate me.' There was also emotional containment needed to enable Sandra to process the events she had experienced when colleagues moved on. This meant Sandra could start to build her resilience levels.

Sandra and her supervisor then began to introduce ways for her to gain some control over her working life (Chapter 6 on stress and coping includes tips on what encourages coping). For Sandra, this meant recognising the autonomy she did have within the workplace and understanding how she could use this to cope better. Stress inoculation skills were used to enable Sandra to take charge of her diary and the time she was spending in each of her roles. By agreeing objectives in both roles she could be clearer about what her priorities were. Sandra and her supervisor then unpicked some of the more difficult work relationships so that she could feel less anxiety about the individuals she worked with. They also developed a plan to move forward.

> **Learning point:** Focusing on strengths and not just areas of concern is an important aspect of emotional containment. This is not done in order to dismiss the current concerns but to enable them to be put into the context of the whole person.

Taking control of your circumstances means not just saying it is the fault of the entire organisation; breaking it down into people and events means you can understand the feelings and their impact further. Is this a personality issue? Is there an individual leader responding to the demands put on them? How can you express to the individuals concerned the impact that this is having on you?

I Zone

As Sandra progressed through the sessions her energy and hopefulness appeared to return. By the end of the individual sessions Sandra was beginning to enter the We Zone. She would talk about work she had done with colleagues, both internal and external to the organisation, and began to see them as a source of support. She was also beginning to develop her approach by identifying individuals in the organisation who could help support her and provide a more balanced view.

The group sessions enabled Sandra to begin to rebuild positive relationships with her group and for them to see her behaviour in a different way.

Case study 2: Matthew, service manager

Matthew is a new service manager. He works with a multidisciplinary team that supports homeless people in a large city.

I Zone

Matthew has only been in his current role for a few months. He entered into the restorative resilience training process with high expectations about how it would support him to develop as a leader. He described wanting to understand the impact of the work on him and to have more insight into the difficulties his team might face. His stress levels were higher than average but he put this down to the responsibilities of the new job. His compassion satisfaction scores were high and burnout in the medium range. His stress levels were being buffered by the pleasure he was taking in his work.

Matthew's emphasis during the sessions was on his desire to learn and be a good manager. He described all of the things he needed to learn and this was experienced by the supervisor as being overwhelming. Matthew was working at full speed on all his projects as he was excited and keen to do a good job. This appeared to be having an effect on the team relationships, as Matthew had not given much thought to how his personal style and desire to 'change the world' was affecting his team.

The supervisor used mirroring and reflecting skills as well as role playing to help Matthew understand the impact of what he was saying. He would often make off-the-cuff remarks about his lack of experience and how he knew nothing.

This was in an attempt to let people know he was keen to learn. Through role play, the supervisor was able to reflect back to Matthew what hearing this was like for a team member who had applied for the role but had not been successful. Together, they were also able to consider the role of a leader and how instilling confidence in those around you was key. By identifying a mentor within the organisation, Matthew was also able to appropriately share his learning needs and act upon them.

Using containment and resilience building, the supervisor was also able to help Matthew to consider why he been successful at gaining this role and what extensive knowledge and skills he already had.

Learning point: Being in a new role can often evoke feelings of anxiety and undermine our ability to work effectively. Reminding Matthew that he was an unfinished product rather than a complete novice was fundamental in building his own confidence as a leader.

No and Why Zone day trips

Although Matthew was clearly in a strong place having recently been promoted, this does not mean that during the sessions he did not have difficult experiences that he wanted to share. These mainly revolved around the behaviour of others towards Matthew and his interpretation of their behaviour as a way to undermine his leadership. For example, on one occasion a team member had raised in front of others during a team meeting how cross he was about not having had his appraisal yet. Matthew had taken this to be a personal challenge. Through the session, the supervisor was able to support Matthew to reflect on why the staff member felt this was important and how he could respond to the individual to establish a positive working relationship rather than simply react.

Matthew's anxiety about his own leadership performance and desire to want to do a good job was at times overwhelming him, and because he was constantly thinking about his role his instructions were not always clear. Slowing his thinking down and reflecting through the sessions was helpful in enabling Matthew to tune in to the staff around him.

We Zone

Matthew began with a positive regard for his employer. What he developed during the session was a better sense of who within the organisation could help him to do what, and how he could contribute to organisational effectiveness himself. The supervisor challenged his understanding through a coaching model, looking at where he wanted to be and the gaps in his knowledge about who could support him. Rather than foster a reliance or dependency on others, Matthew turned this learning into a reciprocal relationship, building strengths, gaining a mentor and ensuring he was well supported in his new role.

During the group sessions Matthew was able to continue to test out his communication skills and develop his understanding of how to lead in an empathetic way.

Case study 3: Amrita, social worker

Amrita is a senior social worker working with adults with learning disabilities.

No and Why Zones

Following a period of excessive change within the organisation, Amrita registered high levels of burnout and stress, and her compassion satisfaction levels were lower than average, suggesting she was struggling to find pleasure in her work.

Amrita described herself as being particularly negative – she had been sent on the training by her manager and she could not think how becoming a supervisor would help her. Amrita became very distressed during her first session and recognised that she was probably her own worst enemy but she felt at the end of her tether. The personal support systems that she had previously relied upon had been eroded following the breakdown of a significant relationship. These events had occurred at the same time as a workplace restructure during which she had been forced to reapply for her job.

The supervisor found Amrita to be difficult and challenging during the initial session, as she vented about her manager and the situation she was in. Amrita went on to describe a difficult serious case review she had been involved in as a result of a deliberate injury to one of the case group she worked with. The entire team had been investigated as a result of the findings and this had come as a blow. It was clear that this had had a significant impact on Amrita and she appeared stuck in these events, questioning why this had happened to her, why the organisation had not been more supportive and what she could have done differently. These events were overshadowed by a consistent theme that Amrita felt she was being unfairly treated.

Rather than trying to change behaviour, the supervisor listened and demonstrated good containment, reflecting back what had happened and the trauma that this had incurred for Amrita. They spent a considerable time in the second session considering the options for Amrita. How she was feeling was clearly impacting on her ability to do her work, and in recognising the significance of the events and the impact they had on Amrita, the supervisor was open with her about the need to process these events in order to move on. Spending time sifting through each detail, getting Amrita to describe the events and what she was thinking and feeling, enabled her to process them in more detail than she had previously.

The experience of telling another person about what was happening and her responses to it appeared to be having a beneficial impact on Amrita, as she started to describe wanting to move beyond these experiences. Despite the detailed accounts, Amrita would sometimes slip back into the events during the sessions. As the supervisor and Amrita had agreed a plan of what they would do if this happened, they were able to note when this occurred and move beyond the experiences to a more productive way of thinking.

Learning point: When significant events have occurred that change our view of the workplace or personal world, they can leave significant markers. The brain is unable to file them away as they are too significant for us. They continue to be replayed in our minds like a tape going over the same events.

I Zone

Once Amrita started to move beyond the overwhelming past experiences, she was able to start to consider what this left her with. Through stress inoculation, the supervisor was able to start to work with Amrita around her stress cognitions. Amrita had a tendency to catastrophise because of previous events. This would manifest as her undermining her own positive plans by constantly thinking things would go terribly wrong. The supervisor was able to work with Amrita to consider the reality of the situation rather than the perceived possible impact.

They then began resilience training, reviewing strengths within the system and thinking about who else was available to draw upon and support the case work. They began to discuss that although the team investigation was traumatic, it also demonstrated the system was working in the best interests of the client and ultimately confirmed that the team were effective. This was a positive outcome of the situation that Amrita had not previously been able to see.

Amrita had not yet entered the We Zone in regards to her organisation, but had started to look at relationships outside of the organisation as sources of support. Her considerable time in the geographical area meant she had a network of personal support from previous workplaces, but she had cut herself off from these people as a result of recent events. Realising the value of these relationships meant that Amrita was motivated to reconnect with colleagues who were important to her. Entering into the group work at this point was also helpful for Amrita in thinking about disclosing vulnerability and getting support from the group.

Chapter 10:
Conclusion

The majority of recommendations that come from serious case reviews and other major enquiries when things go wrong focus on the need to change the work environment or the way in which things are done. This reader argues that undertaking complex helping or caring work will *always* create an environment that is uncertain and where risks are high. We should focus our energies on the individual professionals and consider how we ensure that despite this environment we protect them to thrive.

Using restorative resilience supervision will ensure that professionals are able to enjoy their job and experience increased compassion satisfaction. It will offer them a protective space, ensuring they can not only reduce their stress and burnout levels but learn lessons and skills to ensure they are inoculated against future stressors.

If we want to continue to attract high quality professionals into the caring and helping professions, we need to ensure that instead of blaming them when things go wrong, we accept that the work brings with it a high level of demand. Our role in supporting professionals is to ensure they have the ongoing resources to excel in this environment.

Further information and training

In order to offer a high quality, sustainable training programme for organisations, we have published an organisational training pack which can be purchased from Pavilion Publishing (see https://www.pavpub.com/restorative-resilience-model-of-supervision-training-pack/).

The author is also able to offer a bespoke training package to ensure that a high quality implementation takes place and the sustainability of the programme remains high. For further information please contact Fiduciam at: info@fiduciam.uk

References

Bakker A & Demerouti E (2006) The job demands-resources model: state of the art. *Journal of Managerial Psychology* **22** 309–328.

Baum A, Revenson T & Singer J (2012) *Handbook of Health Psychology*. Hove: Psychology Press.

Begat I & Severinsson E (2006) Reflection on how clinical nursing supervision enhances nurses' experiences of well-being related to their psychosocial work environment. *Journal of Nursing Management* **14** (8) 610–616.

Bennett H & Durkin M (2000) The effects of organisational change on employee psychological attachment: an exploratory study. *Journal of Managerial Psychology* **15** (2) 126–146.

Blake H, Malik S, Mo PK & Pisano C (2011) Do as I say, but not as I do: are next generation nurses role models for health? *Perspectives in Public Health* **131** (5) 231–239.

Bogossian F, Hepworth J, Leong G, Flaws D, Gibbons K, Benefer C & Turner C (2012) A cross-sectional analysis of patterns of obesity in a cohort of working nurses and midwives in Australia, New Zealand, and the United Kingdom. *International Journal of Nursing Studies* **49** 727–738.

British Psychological Society (2008) *Generic Professional Practice Guidelines* (2nd edition). Leicester: BPS.

Brocki J & Wearden A (2005) A critical evaluation of the use of interpretive phenomenological analysis (IPA) in health psychology. *Psychology and Health* **21** (1) 87–108.

Buus N & Gonge H (2009) Empirical studies of clinical supervision in psychiatric nursing: a systematic literature review and methodological critique. *International Journal of Mental Health Nursing* **18** (4) 250–264.

Collins Dictionary (2014) http://www.collinsdictionary.com/dictionary/english/supervise (accessed February 2016).

Colman A (2001) *A Dictionary of Psychology*. Oxford: Oxford University Press.

Coventry LSCB (2013) *Final Overview Report of the Serious Case Review Re: Daniel Pelka*. Coventry: Local Safeguarding Children Board.

Curtis P, Ball L & Kirkham M (2006) Why do midwives leave? (Not) being the kind of midwife you want to be. *British Journal of Midwifery* **14** (1) 27–31.

Cutcliffe J & Hyrkäs K (2006) Multidisciplinary attitudinal positions regarding clinical supervision: a cross-sectional study. *Journal of Nursing Management* **14** (8) 617–627.

DCSF (2009) *The Protection of Children in England: A progress report*. London: TSO.

Department of Health (1993) *A Vision for the Future: The nursing, midwifery and health visiting contribution to health and health care*. London: HMSO.

Department of Health (2013) *Using Restorative Supervision to Improve Clinical Practice and Safeguarding Decisions* [online]. Available at: https://www.gov.uk/government/uploads/system/uploads/attachment_data/file/209911/S15_Restorative_Supervision_Surrey_EISCS_V121211.pdf (accessed February 2016).

D'Souza F, Egan SJ & Rees CS (2011) The relationship between perfectionism, stress and burnout in clinical psychologists. *Behaviour Change* **28** (1) 17–28.

Figley C (1995) *Compassion Fatigue: Coping with secondary traumatic stress in those who treat the traumatized*. New York: Brunner/Mazel.

Firth-Cozens J & Payne R (Eds) (1999) *Stress in Health Professionals: Psychological and organizational causes and inventions*. Chichester: John Wiley & Sons.

Francis R (2013) *Report of the Mid Staffordshire NHS Foundation Trust Public Enquiry*. London: HMSO.

Gonge H & Buus N (2011) Model for investigating the benefits of clinical supervision in psychiatric nursing: a survey study. *International Journal of Mental Health Nursing* **20** (2) 102–111.

Harr C (2013) Promoting workplace health by diminishing the negative impact of compassion fatigue and increasing compassion satisfaction. *Social Work and Christianity* **40** (1) 71–88.

Hochschild A (1983) *The Managed Heart: Commercialization of human feeling*. Berkeley, CA: University of California Press.

Horowitz M (1982) Stress response syndromes and their treatment. In: L Goldberger and S Breznitz (Eds) *Handbook of Stress: Theoretical and clinical aspects* (pp711–732). New York: Free Press.

Howard F (2008) Managing stress or enhancing wellbeing? Positive psychology's contributions to clinical supervision. *Australian Psychologist* **43** 105–113.

Huffington A (2014) *Thrive*. London: Ebury Publishing.

Jones A (2006) Clinical supervision: what do we know and what do we need to know? A review and commentary. *Journal of Nursing Management* **14** (8) 577–585.

Kadushin A (1992) *Clinical Supervisor*. London: Haworth Press.

Kahneman D (2011) *Thinking, Fast and Slow*. London: Penguin.

Keuler D & Safer M (1999) Memory bias in the assessment and recall of pre-exam anxiety: how anxious was I? *Applied Cognitive Psychology* **12** 127–137.

Kihye H, Trinkoff A, Storr C, Geiger-Brown J, Johnson K & Park S (2012) Comparison of job stress and obesity in nurses with favorable and unfavorable work schedules. *Journal of Occupational and Environmental Medicine* **54** (8) 928–932.

Lacy JW & Stark CE (2013). The neuroscience of memory: Implications for the courtroom. *Nature Reviews Neuroscience* **14** (9) 649–658.

Lazarus R & Folkman S (1984) *Stress, Appraisal and Coping*. Oxford: Springer Publishing.

Lea V, Corlett S & Rodgers R (2012) Workload and its impact on community pharmacists' job satisfaction and stress: a review of the literature. *International Journal of Pharmacy Practice* **20** 259–271.

Martin RA, Puhlik-Doris A, Larsen G, Gray J & Weir K (2003) Individual differences in uses of humor and their relation to psychological well-being: development of the Humour Styles Questionnaire. *Journal of Research in Personality* **37** (1) 48–75.

Menzies-Lyth I (1959) The functions of social systems as a defence against anxiety: a report on a study of the nursing service of a general hospital, *Human Relations* **13** 95–121; reprinted in *Containing Anxiety in Institutions: Selected essays, volume 1* (pp43–88). Free Association Books, 1988.

Meyer J & Herscovitch L (2001) Commitment in the workplace: toward a general model. *Human Resource Management* **11** 299–326.

NHS Employers (2009) *Stress Management* [online]. Available at: www.nhsemployers.org/~/media/Employers/Publications/Stress%20management.pdf (accessed February 2016).

Oxford English Dictionary (2015) *Resilience* [online]. Available at: www.oxforddictionaries.com/definition/english/resilience (accessed February 2016).

Pardess E, Mikulincer M, Dekel R & Shaver P (2014) Dispositional attachment orientations, contextual variations in attachment security, and compassion fatigue among volunteers working with traumatized individuals. *Journal of Personality* **82** (5) 355–366.

Paterson HM, Whittle K & Kemp RI (2015) Detrimental effects of post-incident debriefing on memory and psychological responses. *Journal of Police and Criminal Psychology* **30** (1) 27–37.

Peacock L (2012) Public sector workers more likely to take 'sickies'. *The Telegraph* [online]. Available at: www.telegraph.co.uk/finance/jobs/hr-news/9266687/Public-sector-workers-more-likely-to-take-sickies.html (accessed December 2015).

Proctor B (1986) Supervision: a co-operative exercise in accountability. In: M Marken and M Payne (Eds) *Enabling and Ensuring: Supervision in practice*. Leicester: National Youth Bureau.

Rayson M (2011) How public sector sickness figures can aid a balanced debate about staff. *The Guardian* [online]. Available at: www.theguardian.com/public-leaders-network/2011/aug/08/public-sector-sickness-figures-debate (accessed February 2016).

Royal College of Nursing (2013) *Response of the Royal College of Nursing* [online]. Available at: http://royalnursing.3cdn.net/c11a136fd716684867_dnm6i60l3.pdf (accessed February 2016).

Royal College of Nursing (2014) *Clinical Supervision: Guidance for Occupational Health Nurses* [online]. Available at: http://www.supervisionandcoaching.com/pdf/page2/CS%20Guidance%20Occupational%20Health%20Nurses%20(RCN%202002).pdf (accessed February 2016).

Sandoval J (1993) Personality and burnout among school psychologists. *Psychology in the Schools* **30** (4) 321–326.

Shanfelt T, Boone S, Tan L, *et al* (2012) Burnout and satisfaction with work-life balance among US physicians relative to the US population. *Archives of Internal Medicine* **172** 1377–1385.

Stamm BH (2008) *The ProQOL* [online]. Available at: www.proqol.org (accessed February 2016).

St Clair L (2000) Organizational attachment: exploring the psychodynamics of the employment relationship. *Management Working Papers* **1**.

Talbott SM (2007) *The Cortisol Connection: Why stress makes you fat and ruins your health-and what you can do about it*. Berkeley, CA: Hunter House.

Trueland J (2013) Breathe new life into your flagging career. *Nursing Standard* **27** 20–22.

Vlachou E & Plagisou L (2011) Clinical supervision as a support tool for nurses. *Nosileftiki* **50** (3) 279–287.

Wallbank S (2010) Effectiveness of individual clinical supervision for midwives and doctors in stress reduction: findings from a pilot study. *Evidence Based Midwifery* **8** 65–70.

Wallbank S (2013) Maintaining professional resilience through group restorative supervision. *Community Practitioner* **86** (8) 26–28.

Wallbank S (2015) Using restorative resilience supervision to support professionals to thrive in *Interprofessional Staff Supervision in Adult Health and Social Care Services*. Hove: Pavilion Publishing.

Wallbank S & Robertson N (2008) Midwife and nurse responses to miscarriage, stillbirth and neonatal death: a critical review of qualitative research. *Evidence Based Midwifery* **6** (3) 100–106.

Wallbank S & Robertson N (2013) Predictors of staff distress in response to professionally experienced miscarriage, stillbirth and neonatal loss: a questionnaire survey. *International Journal of Nursing Studies* **50** (8) 1090–1097.

Wallbank S & Woods G (2012) A healthier health visiting workforce: findings from the Restorative Supervision Programme. *Community Practitioner* **85** (11) 20–23.

Wang XS, Armstrong MEG, Cairns BG, Key TJ & Travis RC (2011) Shift work and chronic disease: the epidemiological evidence. *Occupational Medicine* **61** (2) 78–89.

Watson D, Clarke LA & Tellegen A (1988) Development and validation of brief measures of positive and negative affect: the PANAS scales. *Journal of Personality and Social Psychology* **54** (6) 1063–1070.

Weiner B (1985) An attributional theory of achievement, motivation and emotion. *Psychological Review* **92** 548–573.

Willemse B, De Jonge J, Smit D, Visser Q, Depla MF & Pot AM (2012) The moderating role of decision authority and co-worker and supervisor support on the impact of job demands in nursing homes: a cross-sectional study. *International Journal of Nursing Studies* **49** 822–833.

Wortman J, Lucas R & Donnellan MB (2012) Stability and change in the Big Five personality domains: evidence from a longitudinal study of Australians. *Psychology and Aging* **27** 867–874.

Wrzesniewski A, McCauley C, Rozin P & Schwartz B (1997) Jobs, careers and callings: people's relations to their work. *Journal of Research in Personality* **31** 21–33.

Further resources from Pavilion Publishing

Interprofessional Staff Supervision in Adult Health and Social Care Services, Volume 1: A Pavilion Annual 2016

Supervising staff from a variety of backgrounds can be challenging. Yet it is an area where practice is ahead of the research since few studies have investigated how best to deliver effective supervision in integrated settings or multidisciplinary teams. What evidence exists tends to focus on services for children, and there is a dearth of information on supervising staff working in adult services.

Part of the new *Learning from Success* series, this first edition explores different models of supervision within adult services, addressing a gap in research and practice about what works when supervising staff from across different professional backgrounds, including social work, nursing, health visiting, clinical psychology, community mental health and addiction services.

This annual helps to support successful supervisory practice by providing readers with a toolkit for supervision in multidisciplinary teams based on research, practice and, unusually, service user perspectives.

Professionals with a wide range of interest can benefit from this resource, including service managers, professionals, front-line health and social care staff, and researchers, providing them with up-to-date research evidence, examples of innovative practice and useful tools and resources to support successful supervision.

Price: £34.95 Order code: E229

Available at: https://www.pavpub.com/interprofessional-staff-supervision-adult-health-social-care-volume-1/

Developing and Supporting Effective Staff Supervision: A training pack to support the delivery of staff supervision training for those working with vulnerable children, adults and their families

Jane Wonnacott

Developed from materials by Tony Morrison

This training pack draws on the core concepts in Tony Morrison's *Staff Supervision in Social Care* (2005) and demonstrates how they can be used to train staff to deliver sound and effective supervision that makes a real difference to service users.

This training pack is for use by experienced trainers who are well grounded in supervision practice and theory. It focuses on training supervisors to deliver one-to-one supervision and its flexible structure enables trainers to design their own bespoke training programmes.

Through group and pair work, participants are actively encouraged to examine and explore their own practice and work together to extend their thinking and improve their skills as supervisors. This pack goes beyond merely teaching theory and actively encourages professional reflection and development.

It is recommended that trainers purchase the associated reader, which gives further detail on supervision theory and provides a good source of preparatory material.

Price: £140

Available at: https://www.pavpub.com/developing-and-supporting-effective-staff-supervision-training-pack/

Developing and Supporting Effective Staff Supervision: A reader to support the delivery of staff supervision training for those working with vulnerable children, adults and their families

Jane Wonnacott

Developed from materials by Tony Morrison

This reader draws on the core concepts in Tony Morrison's *Staff Supervision in Social Care* (2005) and demonstrates how they can be used to train staff to deliver sound and effective supervision that makes a real difference to service users. This reader accompanies the training pack of the same name and is for use by experienced trainers who are well grounded in supervision practice and theory. The reader gives further detail on supervision theory and provides a good source of preparatory material.

The supervision model and accompanying tools have always been designed to enable practitioners to respond to the individual nature of the issues they are working with and create a reflective space for exploring challenging issues and ideas, using the knowledge generated through the process to inform both front-line practice and the strategic direction of the organisation.

Price: £15.95

Available at: https://www.pavpub.com/developing-and-supporting-effective-staff-supervision-handbook/

Supervision for Early Years Workers: A guide for early years professionals about the requirements of supervision

Jane Wonnacott and Penny Sturt

This guide will support early years providers in the delivery of effective staff supervision. Although the Early Years Foundation Stage (EYFS) sets out the framework of expectations in relation to supervision, there are still many differing ideas as to what good supervision looks like in practice and how this can be provided by a busy early years manager. This guide address these fundamental questions:

■ Why is supervision so important?

■ What are the core components of supervision?

■ How can a supervisor and supervisee work together to make supervision effective?

Price: £14.95

Available at: https://www.pavpub.com/supervision-for-early-years-workers/

Staff Supervision in Social Care: Making a real difference for staff and service users

Tony Morrison

This substantial manual contains vital information for anyone involved in supervising, coaching, mentoring or assessing trainees, students and staff involved in delivering or managing services in health, social care, education welfare and community justice settings. The resource contains accessible theory and frameworks with illustrations, examples, diagrams and summaries, photocopiable exercises, checklists and questionnaires.

Price £55

Available at: https://www.pavpub.com/staff-supervision-in-social-care/

Strength to Strength: A facilitator's guide to preparing supervisees, students and trainees for supervision

Tony Morrison

A flexible, session-based resource for facilitators to inform, enhance and accelerate the capacity of supervisees to make maximum use of the supervision process. Improving the contribution to the supervision process, this resource contains guidance for facilitators, development tools and exercises, checklists and additional resources. It contains vital information for trainers and supervisors of trainees, students and staff involved in delivering or managing services in health, social care, education welfare and community justice settings.

Price: £65

Available at: https://www.pavpub.com/strength-to-strength/